Panama Travel Guide 2024-2025

Exploring Natural wonders, Rich Culture, and Modern Marvels in the Heart of Central America

Gina B. Barton

All rights reserved. No part of this publication may be reproduced, distributed, or transmitted in any form or by any means, including photocopying, recording, or other electronic or mechanical methods, without the prior written permission of the publisher, except in the case of brief quotations embodied in critical reviews and certain other noncommercial uses permitted by copyright law.

Copyright © Gina B. Barton, 2024.

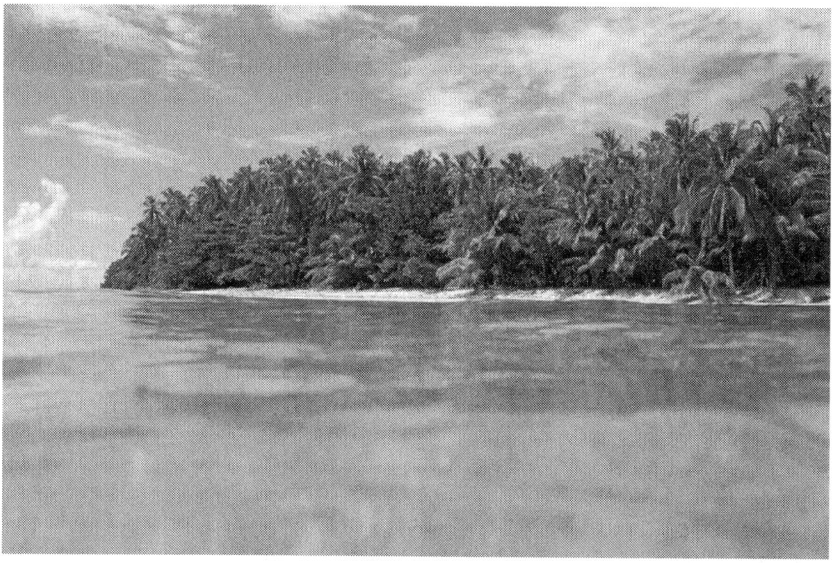

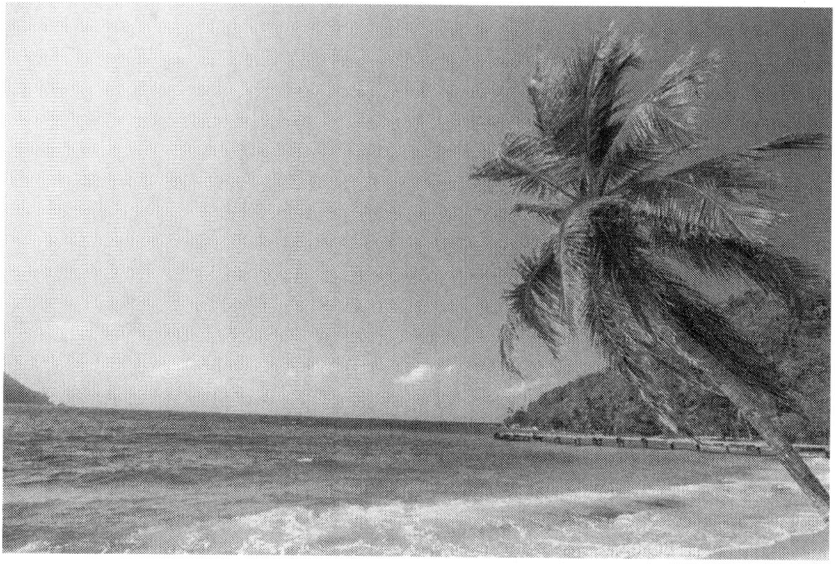

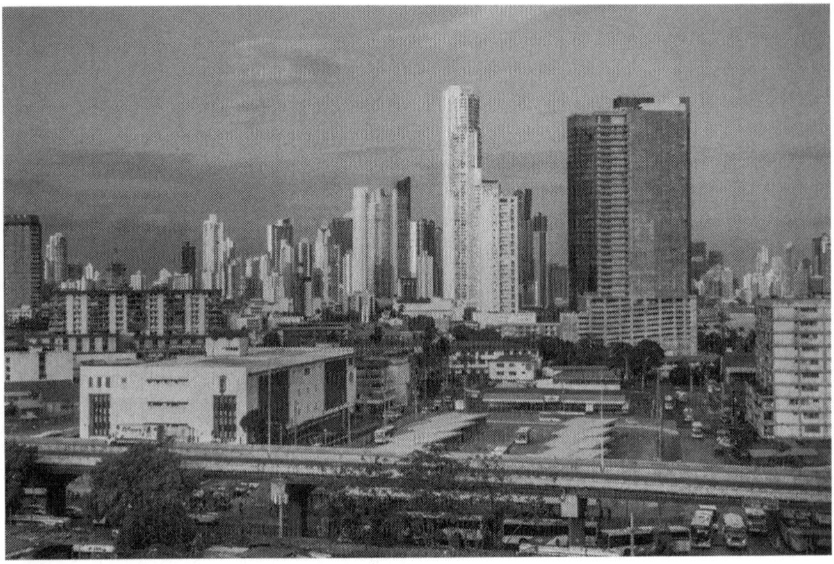

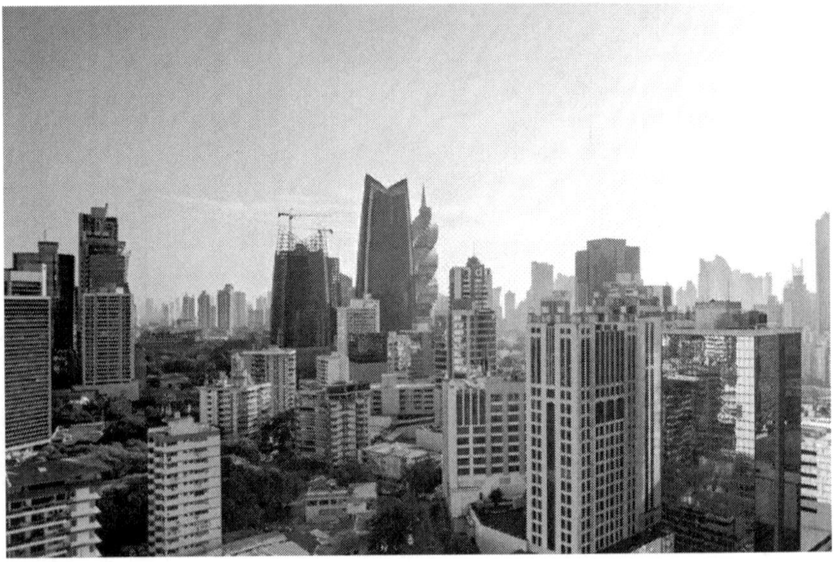

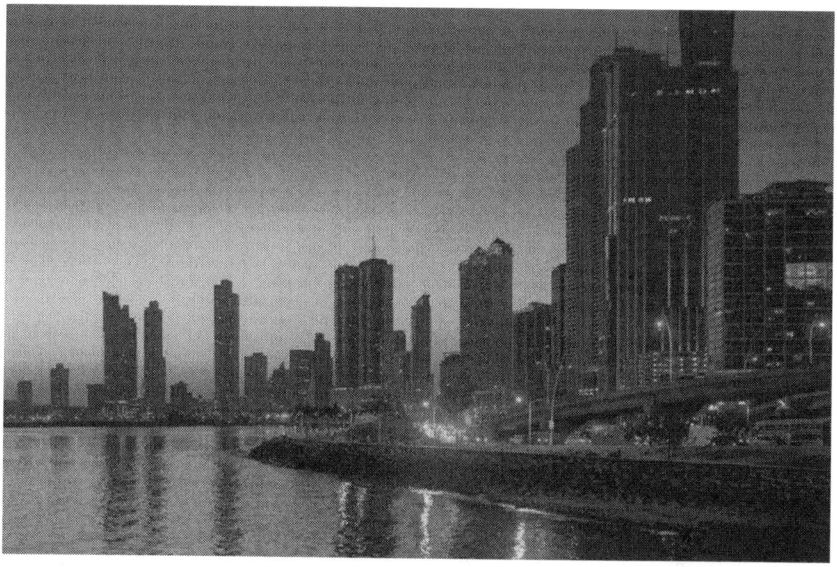

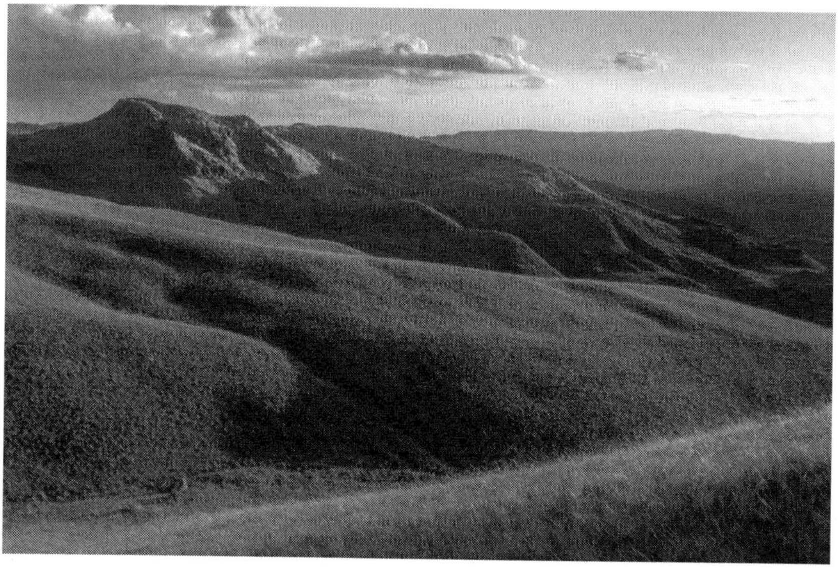

Scan QR Codes with Phone Device to View Maps for Easy Navigation

Table of Contents

INTRODUCTION: A VISIT TO PANAMA 8
- Why Visit Panama 14
- Best Time to Visit 19

CHAPTER 1. PLANNING YOUR TRIP 24
- Entry Requirements and Visas 24
- Getting There and Around 29
- Accommodation Options 38
- Health and Safety 45
- Budgeting for Your Trip 52

CHAPTER 2: PANAMA CITY: THE COSMOPOLITAN HUB 60
- Exploring the Old Town (Casco Viejo) 60
- Modern Panama and Its Skyscrapers 67
- The Panama Canal: A Marvel of Engineering 75
- Top Museums and Cultural Sites 81
- Dining and Nightlife Scene 88

CHAPTER 3: BEYOND THE CAPITAL: REGIONS AND HIGHLIGHTS 96
- The Caribbean Coast 96
- The Pacific Coast 103
- Central Provinces 111
- Chiriquí Highlands 119
- San Blas Islands and Guna Yala 127

CHAPTER 4: ADVENTURES IN NATURE 136
- National Parks and Wildlife Reserves 136
- Hiking and Birdwatching 143
- Water Sports and Beach Activities 150

CHAPTER 5: CULTURAL IMMERSION 156
- Indigenous Communities 156
- Festivals and Events 162
- Panamanian Cuisine 168
- Arts and Crafts 174

CHAPTER 6: ITINERARIES: EXPLORING PANAMA 180
- 3-Day Panama City Stopover 180
- 7-Day Panama Highlights Tour 186

CHAPTER 7: PRACTICAL INFORMATION 194
- Language Tips 194
- Money Matters 199
- Communication and Internet 204
- Packing Essentials 209
- Responsible Travel Tips 215

CHAPTER 8: OFF THE BEATEN PATH 222
- Hidden Gems 222
- Volunteer Opportunities 227
- Unique Experiences 233

CONCLUSION: EMBRACING THE SPIRIT OF PANAMA 238

Introduction: A Visit to Panama

The humid air hit me like a wall as I stepped off the plane in Panama City. It was 2 a.m., and I had no idea where I'd sleep that night. This wasn't how I typically traveled, but a last-minute decision and a cheap flight had landed me in this vibrant Central American country with nothing but a backpack and a vague notion of adventure.

Stumbling through customs, bleary-eyed and jet-lagged, I fumbled with my phone, hoping to find a hostel with a bed available. No luck. The airport Wi-Fi was painfully slow, and my data plan had decided to take a vacation of its own. Great start, right?

But then, something unexpected happened. A friendly face appeared – Jorge, the taxi driver who'd been watching me struggle. "First time in Panama?" he asked with a grin. When I nodded, he waved off my attempts to check my phone. "I know a place. Good price, safe for tourists. You trust me?"

Normally, I'd hesitate. But there was something genuine about Jorge's smile that put me at ease. Plus, what other choice did I have? I climbed into his cab, and we set off into the neon-lit night of Panama City.

As we drove, Jorge became my impromptu tour guide. He pointed out landmarks, shared stories of growing up in the city, and even gave me a crash course in Panamanian slang. By the time we reached the small, family-run hostel he'd recommended, I felt like I'd already gotten a taste of Panama's legendary hospitality.

The next morning, fueled by strong Panamanian coffee and a belly full of fresh fruit, I set out to explore. Without a plan, I let my feet and curiosity guide me. I found myself in Casco Viejo, the old quarter, where colorful colonial buildings stood in stark contrast to the modern skyscrapers on the horizon. Street vendors called out their wares, the scent of grilling meat filled the air, and music seemed to pour from every open window.

A group of locals, noticing my obvious tourist gawking, waved me over. Before I knew it, I was sitting with them, sharing a plate of patacones (fried plantains) and listening to their animated debate about the best place to watch the sunset in the city. Their English was limited, and my Spanish was worse, but laughter bridged the gap.

As the day wore on, one of my new friends, Maria, insisted on showing me her favorite hidden gem — a tiny hole-in-the-wall restaurant where the ceviche was "to die for." She wasn't wrong. As we sat there, savoring the tangy seafood and cold beers, Maria shared stories of her grandmother, who'd worked on the Panama Canal during its expansion. The pride in her voice was palpable, and I found myself eager to learn more about this engineering marvel that had shaped the country's history.

The next few days flew by in a blur of spontaneity and discovery. I hitched a ride with a group of backpackers to the stunning San Blas Islands, where I slept in a hammock under the stars and learned to fish from Guna Yala indigenous people. Their connection to the land and sea was profound, and it made me reflect on my own relationship with nature.

Back in the city, I stumbled upon a local festival in a neighborhood park. Children ran around with painted faces, elderly couples danced to live music, and the air was thick with the smell of barbecue. A grandmother, seeing me standing awkwardly on the sidelines, pulled me into a dance. I was terrible, but her laughter was infectious, and soon I was twirling and stumbling with abandon, surrounded by new friends.

One afternoon, while trying to find my way to a museum, I got hopelessly lost in a residential area. Frustrated and hot, I was about to give up when an elderly man called out to me from his porch. In broken English, he asked if I needed help. When I explained where I was trying to go, he didn't just give me directions – he insisted on walking me there himself. Along the way, he pointed out his favorite local shops and restaurants, giving me insider tips I'd never have found in any guidebook.

As my unplanned week in Panama came to an end, I realized something profound. The best experiences hadn't come from ticking off a list of tourist attractions. They had come from the unexpected encounters, the wrong turns, and most importantly, the incredible warmth of the Panamanian people.

My heart was heavy with memories as I departed, and I vowed to come back. But I also left with a mission. I wanted others to experience the magic of Panama the way I had – with open eyes, an open heart, and a willingness to embrace the unexpected.

That's where this guide comes in. It's not just a collection of facts and must-see sights (though you'll find those too). It's a invitation to discover Panama in all its unscripted glory. We'll give you the tools to explore safely and respectfully, but we'll also encourage you to venture off the beaten path, to say yes to invitations, and to let serendipity be your guide sometimes.

In these pages, you'll find practical advice on everything from navigating the bustling markets of Panama City to choosing the perfect beach for your sunset swim. We'll introduce you to the rich tapestry of Panamanian culture, from the indigenous communities of the rainforest to the Afro-Caribbean flavors of Colón.

You'll learn about Panama's incredible biodiversity and how to experience it responsibly. We'll guide you through the process of witnessing ships pass through the famous canal and explain why this waterway is so much more than just an engineering feat – it's the lifeblood of the nation.

But beyond the practicalities, this guide aims to capture the spirit of Panama – the warmth of its people, the rhythm of its music, the flavors of its cuisine, and the beauty of its landscapes. We'll share stories from locals and long-term expats, giving you insider perspectives on what makes this country truly special.

Whether you're planning a whirlwind weekend in Panama City or a month-long exploration of the country's hidden corners, this guide is your companion. Use it to plan, to dream, and to discover. But remember, the best experiences often come when you put the book down and simply engage with the world around you.

Gather your sense of adventure, brush up on your Spanish (or don't – Panamanians are patient and appreciative of any attempt), and get ready for an unforgettable journey. Panama is waiting to surprise you, just as it surprised me on that fateful unplanned trip.

From the bustling streets of the capital to the tranquil beaches of Bocas del Toro, from the misty highlands of Boquete to the vibrant coral reefs of Coiba, Panama is a country of incredible diversity and endless discovery. It's a place where you can dance until dawn in a city club one day and wake up to the sound of howler monkeys in a rainforest the next.

But most of all, it's a place where strangers become friends, where every meal is an adventure, and where the beauty of the unexpected is always just around the corner. So come with an open mind and a ready smile. Panama is ready to welcome you, just as it welcomed me.

Why Visit Panama

Panama beckons with a siren call that's hard to resist. This narrow strip of land, bridging two continents and two oceans, packs an incredible punch for its size. It's a country where ancient rainforests stand in the shadow of gleaming skyscrapers, where you can sip coffee grown in volcanic soil while watching massive ships traverse an engineering marvel. Panama is a land of contrasts and surprises, waiting to be discovered.

Let's dive into what makes Panama truly special:

1. A Crossroads of Cultures

Panama isn't just a geographical bridge; it's a cultural melting pot. Here, you'll find a vibrant mix of indigenous traditions, Spanish colonial influence, African rhythms, and modern cosmopolitan flair. Walk through the cobblestone streets of Casco Viejo in Panama City, and you'll feel like you've stepped back in time. Colorful colonial buildings house chic boutiques and rooftop bars, where you can sip craft cocktails while gazing at the glittering skyline across the bay.

But venture just a few hours outside the capital, and you might find yourself in a Guna Yala village, where indigenous women still wear traditional mola blouses and paint their faces with geometric designs. Or perhaps you'll end up at a street party in Colón, moving your hips to the Afro-Panamanian rhythms of congo music.

This cultural diversity isn't just something to observe — it's something to experience. You'll taste it in the fusion cuisine that blends tropical ingredients with global influences. You'll hear it in the mix of Spanish, English, and indigenous languages spoken on the streets. And you'll feel it in the warm welcome you receive from Panamanians of all backgrounds.

2. Nature's Playground

Anyone looking for a paradise for adventurers and environment enthusiasts should visit Panama. Despite its small size, it boasts an incredible diversity of ecosystems.

You can start your day spotting resplendent quetzals in the misty cloud forests of Boquete, then end it watching sea turtles nest on a Caribbean beach.

The country is home to over 975 bird species – more than the USA and Canada combined. It's a birdwatcher's dream, with opportunities to spot exotic species like the harpy eagle or the keel-billed toucan.

Marine enthusiasts will find the waters around Panama teeming with possibilities. Snorkel alongside colorful reef fish in the crystal-clear waters of Bocas del Toro. Dive with hammerhead sharks off Coiba Island. Or take a whale-watching tour in the Gulf of Chiriquí, where humpback whales from both hemispheres come to breed.

And let's not forget the rainforests. These lush, green wonderlands cover nearly 40% of the country. Here, you can trek through pristine jungle, spotting howler monkeys, sloths, and if you're lucky, maybe even a elusive jaguar.

3. The Panama Canal: A Marvel of Human Ingenuity

Seeing the Panama Canal is an essential part of every Panama vacation. This 50-mile waterway isn't just an impressive feat of engineering – it's the beating heart of the country, a symbol of Panama's strategic importance in global trade.

Watching a massive container ship squeeze through the narrow locks is a truly awe-inspiring sight. But the canal is more than just a spectator sport. You can kayak on Gatun Lake, part of the canal system, paddling past jungle-covered islands that were once hilltops before the area was flooded.

For history buffs, the canal offers a fascinating glimpse into Panama's past. From the failed French attempt to the successful American project, from the years of U.S. control to the final handover to Panama, the canal's story is intertwined with the country's journey to independence and self-determination.

4. Pristine Beaches and Idyllic Islands

With coastlines on both the Caribbean Sea and the Pacific Ocean, Panama offers a beach for every mood. Want to surf world-class waves? Head to Santa Catalina on the Pacific coast. Dreaming of postcard-perfect white sand and turquoise water? The San Blas Islands in the Caribbean will take your breath away.

Panama's beaches aren't just about sun and sand. They're gateways to adventure. Go sport fishing in the rich waters off Piñas Bay. Spot dolphins and whales off the coast of the Pearl Islands. Or simply sway in a hammock on a deserted island, feeling like you've discovered your own private paradise.

5. A Modern Hub with Deep Roots

Panama City exemplifies the country's unique blend of old and new. It's a major business center, with a skyline that rivals any global metropolis. But amidst the glass and steel towers, you'll find pockets of history and culture.

Stroll through the ruins of Panama Viejo, the original city founded in 1519 and destroyed by pirates in 1671. Then hop over to Casco Viejo, the charming old quarter that rose from the ashes of the original city. Here, historic buildings are being lovingly restored, housing some of the city's hippest restaurants, bars, and boutique hotels.

This juxtaposition of ancient and modern makes Panama an exciting destination for all types of travelers. Whether you're here for business or pleasure, you'll find a country that honors its past while eagerly embracing the future.

Best Time to Visit

Panama's allure is year-round, but timing your visit can make a world of difference. This tropical paradise dances to the rhythm of two seasons: dry and wet. Yet, each month brings its own flavor, from wildlife spectacles to vibrant festivals. Let's journey through Panama's calendar, exploring the best times to experience this captivating country.

Dry Season (December to April):

The dry season is Panama's golden time. From December to April, the sun reigns supreme, painting the sky in brilliant blues. It's the perfect weather for beach lounging, jungle trekking, and city exploring. However, this popularity comes at a price – expect higher rates and larger crowds, especially around Christmas, New Year's, and Easter.

December kicks off the festivities. Panama City buzzes with holiday cheer, its modern skyline twinkling with Christmas lights. The scent of tamales and rum-spiked eggnog fills the air. New Year's Eve is a spectacle, with fireworks illuminating the capital's sky and beach parties rocking until dawn.

January and February are ideal for wildlife enthusiasts. In Bocas del Toro, watch as thousands of dryas butterflies take flight in a mesmerizing orange cloud. It's also prime time for whale watching in the Gulf of Chiriquí, where humpbacks from the southern hemisphere come to breed.

March brings the Feria de las Flores y del Café to Boquete. This ten-day extravaganza celebrates the region's flowers and coffee. Imagine strolling through gardens bursting with orchids, the rich aroma of freshly brewed coffee wafting through the air. It's a feast for the senses.

April marks the end of the dry season with a bang. The Semana Santa (Holy Week) processions in rural areas are a sight to behold, with elaborate religious floats and passionate participants. In Panama City, the heat reaches its peak, making it the perfect time to escape to the breezy beaches of San Blas or the cool mountains of El Valle.

Wet Season (May to November):

Don't let the term "wet season" fool you. While afternoon showers are common, they rarely last long. The rain brings a refreshing coolness and paints the landscapes in vivid greens. It's a time of renewal, when Panama's incredible biodiversity truly shines.

May is a month of transition. The first rains transform the parched landscapes, and wildlife becomes more active. It's an excellent time for birdwatching, as many species begin their mating rituals. In Portobelo, the

Festival de Diablos y Congos erupts in a riot of color and rhythm, celebrating Afro-Panamanian culture.

June and July offer a mix of sun and rain. The brief showers provide welcome relief from the heat, perfect for exploring Panama City's museums or enjoying long lunches in Casco Viejo's charming restaurants. On the Caribbean coast, watch as thousands of sea turtles come ashore to nest – a truly magical experience.

August brings Independence Day celebrations. The streets come alive with parades, folk dances, and the rhythmic beats of drums. It's a fantastic time to immerse yourself in Panamanian culture and pride.

September and October are the wettest months, but they have their own charm. The increased rainfall creates spectacular waterfalls in the highlands, perfect for canyoning adventures. It's also when the famous golden frogs emerge in El Valle de Antón, a rare sight that draws nature lovers from around the world.

November marks the end of the rainy season and the beginning of a month-long celebration of Panamanian identity. The country erupts in a series of independence-related holidays, with parades, traditional dress, and fireworks. It's a time when national pride is on full display, and visitors can't help but get swept up in the excitement.

Year-Round Considerations:

While seasonal patterns generally hold true, Panama's diverse microclimates mean you can often find good weather somewhere in the country at any time. The Caribbean coast, for instance, can experience rain year-round but also periods of sunshine during the wet season.

Panama's position near the equator means daylight hours remain relatively constant throughout the year. You can count on about 12 hours of daylight, with the sun rising around 6 AM and setting around 6 PM. This consistency makes it easier to plan outdoor activities, regardless of when you visit.

Temperature variations are more noticeable based on elevation rather than season. While coastal areas stay warm year-round, the highlands offer cool relief. Boquete, nestled in the mountains, can see temperatures drop to the low 60s°F (around 16°C) at night, even when the lowlands are sweltering.

Ultimately, the best time to visit Panama depends on your interests. Wildlife enthusiasts might prefer the wet season when the forests are lush and animals are active. Beach lovers might opt for the dry season's guaranteed sunshine. Culture vultures could time their visit to coincide with one of the many festivals.

No matter when you choose to visit, Panama promises an unforgettable experience. From the bustling streets of

Panama City to the tranquil beaches of Bocas del Toro, from the misty cloud forests of Chiriquí to the historic forts of Portobelo, every season reveals a new facet of this diverse and captivating country. So pack your bags, bring your sense of adventure, and prepare to fall in love with Panama, whatever the weather.

Chapter 1. Planning Your Trip

Entry Requirements and Visas

Planning a trip to Panama is exciting, but understanding the entry requirements and visa policies is crucial for a smooth journey. The good news? Panama's entry procedures are relatively straightforward for many travelers. However, it's important to note that regulations can change, so always check with official sources before your trip.

Let's start with the basics. Many visitors to Panama, especially tourists from North America and Europe, benefit from Panama's welcoming visa policy. Citizens of countries like the United States, Canada, most European Union nations, Australia, New Zealand, and several others can enter Panama without a visa for stays up to 180 days. This generous policy allows for extended exploration of the country's diverse regions, from the bustling streets of Panama City to the pristine beaches of Bocas del Toro.

But don't get too excited just yet – there are still important requirements to meet. All visitors must have a passport valid for at least three months beyond their intended stay. It's also crucial to have proof of onward travel, showing that you plan to leave Panama within the allowed timeframe. This ticket may be for one way travel or it may be for your next stop. Without this, you might face issues at the border or even be denied entry.

Financial proof is another key requirement. Panama wants to ensure that visitors can support themselves during their stay. While there's no specific amount stipulated, it's wise to have access to sufficient funds or a valid credit card. Being prepared with bank statements or credit card information can save you from potential headaches at immigration.

Now, let's talk about the tourist card. Many visitors who don't need a visa will instead receive a tourist card upon arrival. This small piece of paper is your official permission to be in Panama, so guard it carefully! It will be required of you when you exit the nation. The tourist card typically costs around 30 USD and can be paid in cash or by credit card at the airport.

But what if you're not from a visa-exempt country? Don't worry – Panama still welcomes you! You'll need to apply for a visa before your trip. The process involves submitting an application to a Panamanian embassy or consulate in your home country. Required documents usually include your passport, passport-sized photos, proof of funds, a return ticket, and sometimes a letter explaining the purpose of your visit.

The visa application process can take anywhere from a few days to several weeks, depending on your nationality and the embassy's workload. It's crucial to start this process well in advance of your planned trip. Nothing dampens travel excitement quite like last-minute visa stress!

Individuals seeking to remain in Panama beyond 180 days or potentially pursue employment opportunities face different regulations. You might need to look into options like the Friendly Nations Visa or various work permit categories. These processes are more complex and often require the assistance of a local lawyer.

It's worth noting that Panama has special agreements with some countries. For instance, citizens of certain Central American nations can enter with just their national ID card under the CA-4 agreement. Always check if any specific arrangements apply to your nationality.

Health requirements are another crucial aspect of entry procedures. While Panama doesn't generally require vaccinations for entry, it's strongly recommended to be up-to-date on routine vaccines. If you're traveling from a country with risk of yellow fever, you may need to show proof of vaccination.

Upon arrival in Panama, be prepared for the immigration process. Lines may be lengthy, particularly during prime tourist seasons. Have all your documents ready – passport, tourist card or visa, proof of onward travel, and any other required paperwork. Immigration officers may ask about your travel plans, so it's helpful to have a general itinerary in mind.

Entry requirements can vary based on your port of arrival. While procedures at Tocumen International Airport in Panama City are usually straightforward, land borders or smaller airports might have different processes. If you're planning to enter through a less common route, it's wise to research specific procedures for that entry point.

One often overlooked aspect of entry requirements is exit procedures. When leaving Panama, you'll need to pay an exit tax. This is often included in airline tickets, but it's worth confirming to avoid surprises at the airport. Land border crossings typically require cash payment of this tax.

For travelers with special circumstances, such as minors traveling alone or individuals with dual citizenship, additional documentation may be necessary. Minors might need notarized permission from both parents, while dual citizens should be aware of which passport to use for entry and exit.

Lastly, it's crucial to respect the terms of your stay in Panama. Overstaying your visa or permitted time can result in fines or even bans on future entry. If you fall in love with Panama (and many do!) and want to extend your stay, make sure to look into extension procedures well before your authorized time runs out.

Navigating entry requirements might seem daunting, but with proper preparation, it's a small hurdle on the way to your Panamanian adventure. Each step brings you closer to experiencing the vibrant culture, stunning landscapes, and warm hospitality that make Panama a truly special destination. So gather your documents, triple-check your requirements, and get ready for an unforgettable journey in this captivating country.

Getting There and Around

Panama beckons with its lush rainforests, pristine beaches, and vibrant culture. Whether you're dreaming of exploring the historic Panama Canal, lounging on sun-soaked Caribbean islands, or immersing yourself in the buzz of Panama City, your journey begins with smart travel planning. Let's explore the best ways to reach this Central American gem and traverse its diverse landscapes.

Major Airports:

Tocumen International Airport (PTY) - Panama City

The country's primary gateway, Tocumen handles over 15 million passengers annually. Located about 24 kilometers east of Panama City, it's a modern facility with plenty of amenities.

Pros:

- Extensive international connections
- Well-equipped with shops, restaurants, and lounges
- Efficient customs and immigration processes

Cons:

- Can be crowded during peak travel seasons
- Distance from the city center means potential traffic delays

Enrique Malek International Airport (DAV) - David

Travelers bound for Boquete or Bocas del Toro will find this airport serving Panama's western region ideal for their journey.

Pros:

- Convenient access to highland and coastal destinations
- Smaller size means quicker processing times

Cons:

- Limited international flights

- Fewer amenities compared to Tocumen

Marcos A. Gelabert International Airport (PAC) - Panama City

Also known as Albrook Airport, it primarily serves domestic routes and some international flights to nearby countries.

Pros:
- Close to Panama City center
- Quick check-in and security processes

Cons:
- Limited flight options
- Smaller terminal with fewer facilities

Airlines:

Copa Airlines

Panama's flag carrier offers extensive connections throughout the Americas.

Pros:
- Extensive network, especially within Latin America
- Modern fleet and good service standards
- Competitive prices on many routes

Cons:
- Limited options for travel to Europe or Asia

- Can be more expensive than budget alternatives on some routes

American Airlines, United, and Delta

These major U.S. carriers provide regular service to Panama from various North American hubs.

Pros:

- Frequent flights from multiple U.S. cities
- Opportunity to earn and redeem miles on large airline alliances
- Often offer competitive fares, especially during sales

Cons:

- May require layovers for travelers outside major hubs
- Service quality can vary

Air France and KLM

These European airlines offer direct flights from Paris and Amsterdam, respectively.

Pros:

- Direct connections from Europe
- High service standards
- Possibility to combine Panama with European destinations

Cons:

- Limited frequency (usually a few times per week)
- Can be pricier than other options

Internal Transportation:

Domestic Flights

Airlines like Air Panama connect major cities and popular tourist destinations.

Pros:

- Quick way to cover large distances
- Time-saving for travelers with limited schedules
- Scenic views of the countryside

Cons:

- More expensive than ground transportation
- Luggage restrictions
- Weather-dependent in some regions

Buses

Panama's bus network is extensive and affordable, connecting most towns and cities.

Pros:

- Budget-friendly option
- Opportunity to see the countryside
- Frequent departures on popular routes

Cons:

- Longer travel times
- Varying levels of comfort
- May not reach more remote areas

Panama Canal Railway

This scenic train ride connects Panama City to Colón along the canal.

Pros:

- Unique experience with beautiful views
- Comfortable, air-conditioned carriages
- Historical significance

Cons:

- Limited schedule (usually one round trip per day)
- Not practical for regular transportation needs
- Relatively expensive for the short journey

Rental Cars

Major international agencies operate in Panama, offering flexibility for explorers.

Pros:

- Freedom to create your own itinerary
- Convenient for reaching off-the-beaten-path destinations
- Can be cost-effective for groups

Cons:

- Challenging driving conditions in some areas
- Parking can be difficult in cities
- Additional costs like insurance and fuel

Taxis and Ride-sharing

Available in major cities and tourist areas, providing convenient point-to-point transport.

Pros:

- Easy to use, especially in urban areas
- There is no need to be concerned about parking or navigation.
- Can be affordable for short trips

Cons:

- Some taxis may not use meters, requiring negotiation
- Safety concerns with unlicensed operators
- Can be expensive for longer journeys

Water Taxis and Ferries

Essential for reaching many of Panama's islands and coastal areas.

Pros:

- Frequently, the sole method of reaching specific locations
- Scenic journeys with potential wildlife sightings
- Part of the authentic Panama experience

Cons:

- Schedules can be limited or weather-dependent
- Diverse levels of protection and convenience
- May not suit travelers prone to seasickness

When planning your Panamanian adventure, consider combining multiple transportation modes to maximize your experience. For instance, you might fly into Panama City, take the scenic train to Colón, then hop on a water taxi to reach a Caribbean island. Or rent a car to explore the highlands of Chiriquí, then catch a domestic flight back to the capital.

Travel times can vary significantly depending on your chosen method and destination. Build some flexibility into your itinerary to account for potential delays or unexpected discoveries along the way.

Ultimately, the joy of traveling in Panama lies not just in the destinations you reach, but in the journeys between them. Each mode of transport offers a unique perspective on this diverse country, from soaring over lush rainforests to chatting with locals on a cross-country bus ride. Embrace the variety, and you'll find that getting there truly is half the fun in Panama.

How to Scan QR Code Maps in This Panama Travel Guide

Follow these simple steps to access and navigate the maps linked via QR codes in this guide:

1. Open Your Camera: Use your smartphone or tablet's camera. If your device doesn't support QR scanning, download a QR code scanner app.

2. Scan the QR Code: Hold your device's camera over the QR code found on the page. Ensure the code is clearly visible on your screen.

3. Tap the Notification: A link should pop up on your screen. Tap it to open the map in your browser.

4. Explore the Map: Use the map to find attractions, plan routes, and navigate Panama with ease.

Now you're ready to make the most of your journey through Panama!

Accommodation Options

Panama's diverse landscapes and vibrant culture are matched by an equally varied array of accommodation options. From the glittering high-rises of Panama City to rustic eco-lodges nestled in the rainforest, travelers can find the perfect place to rest their heads after days filled with adventure. Let's explore the rich tapestry of lodging choices awaiting you in this captivating Central American nation.

Luxury Hotels:

In Panama City, luxury hotels reach for the sky, offering unparalleled views and world-class amenities. Within the city, the Waldorf Astoria Panama is a shining example of luxury. With its sleek, modern design and impeccable service, it caters to discerning travelers seeking the finer things in life. Guests can indulge in spa treatments, savor gourmet cuisine, and unwind in spacious suites adorned with elegant furnishings. Located at 47th Street & Uruguay Street, this five-star establishment is easily accessible from the bustling financial district and is just a short drive from Tocumen International Airport. For reservations, call +507 294-8000.

Venturing to the Pacific coast, the Buenaventura Golf & Beach Resort offers a different flavor of luxury. Spread across a vast property dotted with lagoons and lush gardens, this JW Marriott resort combines colonial-inspired architecture with modern comforts. Golf enthusiasts will relish the 18-hole Jack Nicklaus-designed course, while beach lovers can bask on the resort's private stretch of sand. With multiple restaurants, a spa, and activities for all ages, it's a self-contained paradise. You'll find this oasis in Río Hato, about two hours' drive from Panama City. Contact them at +507 908-3333 to book your stay.

Boutique Hotels:

For travelers seeking more intimate accommodations with personalized touches, Panama's boutique hotel scene is burgeoning. In the historic Casco Viejo district of Panama City, La Concordia Boutique Hotel captures the essence of old-world charm fused with contemporary luxury. Housed in a lovingly restored colonial building, each of its 10 rooms tells a unique story through carefully curated décor and locally sourced artwork. The rooftop bar offers breathtaking views of the Panama City skyline, perfect for sipping cocktails as the sun sets. Located at Avenida B and Calle 8, this gem is within walking distance of Casco Viejo's main attractions. Reach out to them at +507 800-1000 to secure your room in this sought-after hotel.

Eco-Lodges:

Panama's commitment to preserving its natural beauty shines through in its eco-lodges. The Yandup Island Lodge in the San Blas archipelago offers an immersive experience in the culture and environment of the Guna Yala indigenous community. Thatched-roof cabanas perch over crystal-clear waters, providing a front-row seat to marine life. Solar power and rainwater collection systems minimize the lodge's environmental impact. Guests can explore nearby islands, snorkel in pristine waters, and learn about Guna traditions. This remote paradise is accessible by a short flight from Panama City to Playon Chico, followed by a boat transfer. For an unforgettable stay, contact them at +507 6641-6765.

In the mist-shrouded mountains of Boquete, Finca Lerida Coffee Plantation and Boutique Hotel combines eco-friendly practices with a deep dive into Panama's coffee culture. Surrounded by cloud forests and coffee plantations, this historic estate offers charming rooms with panoramic views. Guests can participate in coffee tours, birdwatching excursions, and hiking trails that wind through the property's lush grounds. The farm-to-table restaurant showcases local ingredients, including coffee from the estate. Located just outside Boquete town, it's easily reached by car or shuttle from David Airport. Make your reservation by calling +507 720-1111.

All-Inclusive Resorts:

For travelers seeking a hassle-free vacation, Panama's all-inclusive resorts deliver sun, sand, and relaxation in generous doses. The Dreams Playa Bonita Panama Resort & Spa, situated just 20 minutes from Panama City, offers a beachfront escape with all the trimmings. Seven restaurants, five bars, and a world-class spa ensure that every whim is catered to. Activities range from non-motorized water sports to Spanish lessons and cooking classes. The resort's location allows for easy day trips to the Panama Canal or the capital's attractions. Nestled in a cove with views of ships entering the canal, it's a picturesque spot to unwind. Dial +507 211-3700 to book your all-inclusive getaway.

Hostels and Budget Accommodations:

Budget-conscious travelers and backpackers will find plenty of wallet-friendly options throughout Panama. In Panama City, Selina Casco Viejo has elevated the hostel concept with its blend of dormitory-style rooms and private accommodations. The colonial building has been transformed into a vibrant social hub, complete with a co-working space, yoga deck, and communal kitchen. Regular events and tours foster a sense of community among guests. Located in the heart of Casco Viejo at Avenida A & Calle 12 Este, it's an ideal base for exploring the old town and beyond. Book your stay by calling +507 838-5137.

Vacation Rentals:

The rise of platforms like Airbnb has opened up a world of unique accommodation options in Panama. From sleek city apartments with skyline views to beachfront villas on the Pacific coast, vacation rentals offer the comforts of home with local flavor. In Bocas del Toro, over-water bungalows available for rent provide an authentic Caribbean experience. These rentals often come with the added benefit of local hosts who can provide insider tips on the best restaurants, hidden beaches, and off-the-beaten-path attractions.

Glamping and Unique Stays:

Adventurers seeking something truly out of the ordinary will find Panama doesn't disappoint. The Canopy Tower in Soberanía National Park transforms a former U.S. military radar tower into a birdwatcher's paradise. Circular rooms offer 360-degree views of the surrounding rainforest canopy, while the observation deck is perfect for spotting toucans, monkeys, and sloths. Located just 45 minutes from Panama City, it's an accessible way to immerse yourself in nature without sacrificing comfort. Reach out to them at +507 264-5720 to book this one-of-a-kind experience.

Choosing the right accommodation can elevate your Panamanian adventure from memorable to truly extraordinary. Whether you're dreaming of falling asleep to the sound of waves lapping at your overwater bungalow, waking up to panoramic views of Panama City's skyline, or being lulled by the calls of howler monkeys in a rainforest lodge, there's a perfect spot waiting for you.

Panama's high season, typically from December to April, sees accommodation prices rise and availability decrease. Booking well in advance for these periods is advisable, especially for popular destinations like Bocas del Toro and Boquete. Conversely, the green season (May to November) often brings lower rates and fewer crowds, though some remote lodges may have limited operations during this time.

When planning a Panamanian odyssey, consider mixing and matching accommodation types to fully experience the country's diversity. Start with a few nights in a luxury Panama City hotel to acclimate and explore urban attractions. Then, venture to an eco-lodge in the rainforest for wildlife encounters and adventure activities. Cap off your trip with a stay at a beachfront resort or a quaint bed and breakfast in a mountain town.

Wherever you choose to rest your head in Panama, you're sure to find warmth, hospitality, and a connection to the incredible landscapes and cultures that make this country so special. From the moment you check in until the bittersweet checkout, your accommodation will be more than just a place to sleep – it will be an integral part of your Panamanian story.

Health and Safety

Embarking on a Panamanian adventure promises excitement, discovery, and unforgettable experiences. However, ensuring your health and safety should be a top priority when planning your journey to this vibrant Central American nation. By taking the right precautions and staying informed, you can focus on enjoying Panama's lush rainforests, pristine beaches, and rich cultural heritage without unnecessary worry.

Vaccinations: Before packing your bags, it's crucial to consult with a travel health professional or your doctor about recommended vaccinations. While Panama is generally safe from a health perspective, certain immunizations can provide extra protection and peace of mind.

Routine Vaccinations: Ensure you're up-to-date on standard vaccinations such as measles-mumps-rubella (MMR), diphtheria-tetanus-pertussis, varicella (chickenpox), polio, and your yearly flu shot. These form the foundation of your travel health preparation.

Hepatitis A: This vaccination is recommended for most travelers. Hepatitis A can be contracted through contaminated food or water, regardless of where you stay or eat. Getting this shot is a smart precaution for exploring Panama's diverse culinary scene with confidence.

Hepatitis B: Consider this vaccination if you plan on getting a tattoo or piercing, or if you might need medical procedures during your stay. It's also advisable for travelers engaging in adventure activities with a risk of injury.

Typhoid: Particularly important if you're planning to venture off the beaten path or explore smaller towns and rural areas. One may get typhoid by drinking or eating tainted food.

Yellow Fever: While not required for entry into Panama, the yellow fever vaccine is recommended for travelers visiting certain areas, particularly the province of Darién. It's also a requirement if you're arriving from a country with risk of yellow fever transmission.

Rabies: If your itinerary includes extensive outdoor activities, working with animals, or visiting remote areas, discussing rabies vaccination with your healthcare provider is wise. While rabies is not common in Panama, it's present in wildlife such as bats and monkeys.

Health Precautions:

Water Safety: While tap water is generally safe to drink in Panama City and other major urban areas, it's prudent to stick to bottled or purified water in rural regions. Ice cubes in reputable establishments in cities are usually safe, but exercise caution in more remote locations.

Food Safety: Panama's culinary scene is a delight, but take sensible precautions. Opt for freshly cooked, hot foods and avoid raw or undercooked meats and seafood. Street food can be tempting and often delicious – use your judgment and choose vendors with high turnover and good hygiene practices.

Sun Protection: Panama's tropical climate means intense sun exposure. Pack broad-spectrum sunscreen with high SPF, wear protective clothing, and don't forget a wide-brimmed hat. The sun can be deceptively strong, even on cloudy days, especially in high-altitude areas like Boquete.

Mosquito-borne Illnesses: While Panama has made great strides in controlling mosquito-borne diseases, it's essential to protect yourself. Use insect repellent containing DEET, wear long-sleeved shirts and pants, and consider treating your clothes with permethrin. If your accommodation doesn't have screens, sleep under a mosquito net, particularly in rural areas.

Altitude Sickness: If your plans include visiting Panama's highlands, such as Boquete or Cerro Punta, be aware of the potential for altitude sickness. Symptoms can include headache, fatigue, and nausea. Acclimatize slowly, stay hydrated, and avoid alcohol in the first 24 hours at high altitudes.

Medical Facilities: Panama City boasts several world-class hospitals and clinics, but medical facilities in rural areas may be limited. Consider obtaining travel insurance that includes medical evacuation. Carry any necessary prescription medications in their original containers, along with a copy of the prescription.

Safety Tips:

Urban Safety: Panama is generally safe for tourists, but like any destination, it's important to stay alert, especially in urban areas. In Panama City, exercise caution in certain neighborhoods after dark. Stick to well-lit, populated areas and use reputable taxi services or ride-sharing apps for night-time transportation.

Petty Crime: While violent crime against tourists is rare, petty theft can occur. Keep valuables secure, be discreet with expensive electronics or jewelry, and use hotel safes when available. When using public transit and in busy tourist destinations, use extra caution.

Beach Safety: Panama's beaches are stunning, but some have strong currents. Always heed local warnings and flag systems. If you're not a confident swimmer, stay on beaches where lifeguards are on duty. Be cautious of marine life – while rare, stingray and jellyfish stings can occur.

Hiking and Jungle Excursions:

When exploring Panama's lush wilderness, go with reputable guides who know the terrain. Inform someone of your plans if heading out independently. Wear appropriate footwear, carry plenty of water, and be prepared for sudden weather changes, especially during the rainy season.

Road Safety: If you're planning to drive in Panama, be prepared for varying road conditions. While major highways are generally well-maintained, rural roads can be challenging, particularly during the rainy season. Always carry a spare tire, water, and emergency supplies. Be cautious of pedestrians and wildlife, especially at night.

Natural Disasters: Panama is largely free from major natural disasters, but it's good to be aware of potential risks. The Pacific coast can experience occasional earthquakes, while heavy rains can lead to flooding and landslides, particularly from May to December. Stay informed about weather conditions and follow local advice during extreme weather events.

Cultural Sensitivity: Respecting local customs and traditions not only enriches your travel experience but also contributes to your safety. Dress modestly when visiting rural areas or indigenous communities. Always ask permission before photographing people, especially in traditional communities.

LGBTQ+ Travelers: Panama is generally tolerant, especially in urban areas and tourist destinations. However, public displays of affection may attract unwanted attention in more conservative regions. Use discretion and research LGBTQ+ friendly establishments and areas.

Wildlife Encounters: Panama's biodiversity is a major draw, but remember that wildlife should be admired from a safe distance. Even if an animal seems friendly, never feed them or approach them. Be particularly cautious of snakes in forested areas – wear closed-toe shoes and stay on marked trails.

Emergency Services: Familiarize yourself with local emergency numbers. In Panama, dial 911 for general emergencies, 103 for the police, and 104 for an ambulance. It's helpful to have these numbers saved in your phone and written down separately.

Travel Insurance: Strongly consider comprehensive travel insurance that covers medical emergencies, trip cancellations, and lost luggage. Ensure it includes coverage for any adventure activities you plan to undertake, such as scuba diving or zip-lining.

Stay Informed: Before and during your trip, check your government's travel advisory website for up-to-date information on Panama. Register with your embassy if possible, especially if venturing to more remote areas.

By taking these health and safety precautions, you're setting the stage for a worry-free exploration of Panama's wonders. From the bustling streets of Panama City to the serene islands of Bocas del Toro, from the historic Panama Canal to the mist-shrouded mountains of Chiriquí, you'll be well-prepared to immerse yourself in the country's diverse landscapes and rich culture. Remember, a little preparation goes a long way in ensuring your Panamanian adventure is filled with nothing but positive memories and incredible experiences.

Budgeting for Your Trip

Planning a trip to Panama is an exciting endeavor, filled with dreams of tropical beaches, lush rainforests, and vibrant culture. However, turning these dreams into reality requires careful financial planning. Whether you're a budget backpacker, a comfort-seeking mid-range traveler, or someone looking for a luxury escape, Panama offers experiences to suit every pocket. Let's break down the costs and create sample budgets for different travel styles to help you plan your perfect Panamanian adventure.

Budget Travel: $30-$50 per day

Embracing budget travel in Panama doesn't mean sacrificing experiences – it's about making smart choices and prioritizing what matters most to you. With careful planning, you can stretch your dollars far and immerse yourself in the local culture.

Accommodation: $10-$15 per night

Budget travelers can find affordable dormitory-style rooms in hostels throughout Panama. In Panama City, places like Luna's Castle in Casco Viejo offer beds for as low as $12 per night. In popular destinations like Bocas del Toro, hostels like Selina offer basic dorm beds starting around $15. These accommodations often provide communal kitchens, allowing you to save money by preparing some of your own meals.

Food: $10-$15 per day

Eating like a local is key to budget travel in Panama. Start your day with a hearty Panamanian breakfast of hojaldras (fried bread) with eggs and coffee for about $3-$4. For lunch and dinner, seek out local fondas (small family-run eateries) where you can enjoy filling meals of rice, beans, and meat for $3-$5. Street food like empanadas or tamales can be found for $1-$2, perfect for snacks or light meals.

Transportation: $5-$10 per day

Panama's public transportation system is affordable and extensive. In Panama City, the metro costs just $0.35 per trip, while city buses charge $0.25. For intercity travel, comfortable express buses connect major destinations at reasonable prices. For example, the journey from Panama City to David (near Boquete) costs around $15-$20 for an 8-hour ride.

Activities: $0-$10 per day

Many of Panama's natural attractions can be enjoyed for free or at a low cost. Hiking in national parks, lounging on beaches, and exploring local markets don't have to cost a dime. When you do want to splurge on a paid activity, look for group tours to share costs. A guided hike in Boquete might cost $30-$40, but it's a worthy occasional splurge to enhance your experience.

Mid-Range Travel: $100-$150 per day

Mid-range travelers in Panama can enjoy a comfortable balance of local experiences and modern conveniences. This budget allows for nicer accommodations, more restaurant meals, and a wider range of activities.

Accommodation: $50-$80 per night

At this price point, you can stay in comfortable hotels or private rooms in upscale hostels. In Panama City, hotels like the Novotel Panama City or Hilton Garden Inn offer rooms starting around $70-$80 per night. In beach destinations like Santa Catalina, charming guesthouses with ocean views can be found for $60-$70.

Food: $25-$35 per day

Mid-range travelers can enjoy a mix of local eateries and more upscale restaurants. Start your day with a leisurely breakfast at a café for $7-$10. For lunch, you might try a trendy spot in Casco Viejo, spending $12-$15 for a meal. Dinners at nice restaurants featuring international cuisine or gourmet Panamanian dishes might cost $20-$30 per person.

Transportation: $15-$25 per day

While you can still use public transportation, this budget allows for more taxis or Uber rides within cities. Renting a car becomes an option, especially when exploring areas like the highlands of Chiriquí. Car rentals start around $30-$40 per day, not including fuel. For longer distances, you might opt for domestic flights to save time – a flight from Panama City to David costs about $100-$150.

Activities: $20-$40 per day

This budget opens up a world of exciting activities. You could take a partial transit tour of the Panama Canal for around $150, enjoy a coffee tour in Boquete for $30, or go snorkeling in Bocas del Toro for $25. Allocating more for activities allows you to fully immerse yourself in Panama's diverse offerings.

Luxury Travel: $250+ per day

Travelers craving the pinnacle of comfort and exclusive experiences will find Panama offers a wealth of luxurious options. This budget allows you to indulge in the finest accommodations, gourmet dining, and bespoke activities.

Accommodation: $150-$300+ per night

Luxury travelers can choose from a range of high-end hotels and resorts. In Panama City, the Waldorf Astoria offers rooms starting at $250 per night, with stunning views of the city skyline. For a beach getaway, the JW Marriott Panama Golf & Beach Resort provides lavish rooms and amenities starting around $300 per night. In Bocas del Toro, over-water bungalows at Eclypse de Mar offer an exclusive retreat for $250-$300 per night.

Food: $70-$100+ per day

Gourmet cuisine takes center stage in the luxury travel experience. Start your day with an elaborate breakfast buffet at your hotel, often included in room rates. For lunch and dinner, explore Panama's fine dining scene. Restaurants like Donde José in Panama City offer innovative tasting menus showcasing local ingredients for around $75-$100 per person. Add in premium wines or cocktails, and your daily food budget can easily reach $100 or more.

Transportation: $50-$100+ per day

Luxury travel often means private transportation for maximum comfort and flexibility. Hiring a private car with a driver costs around $100-$150 per day. For longer distances, private domestic flights or helicopter transfers provide a stylish and time-efficient option. A private charter flight from Panama City to Bocas del Toro might cost $500-$1000, depending on the aircraft.

Activities: $100-$200+ per day

The sky's the limit when it comes to luxury experiences in Panama. Enjoy a private yacht tour around the Pearl Islands for $500-$1000 per day. Take a helicopter tour over the Panama Canal and rainforest for $300-$500 per person. Indulge in a full-day spa package at a luxury resort for $200-$300. For wildlife enthusiasts, a private guided tour in Soberanía National Park with an expert naturalist can cost $200-$300.

Additional Considerations:

Seasonal Variations: Depending on the season, prices may change. The dry season (December to April) is generally more expensive, especially around holidays. Traveling during the green season (May to November) can offer significant savings, even on luxury accommodations.

Special Experiences: Regardless of your overall budget, consider allocating funds for one or two special experiences that resonate with your interests. Whether it's a scenic flight over the Darién Gap or a multi-day sailing trip in the San Blas Islands, these unique activities often become the highlights of a trip.

Tipping: Remember to factor in tips for guides, drivers, and service staff. In Panama, 10% is standard in restaurants (often already included in the bill), while tour guides generally expect 10-15% for good service.

Emergency Fund: Always set aside a portion of your budget for unexpected expenses or spontaneous opportunities. Having this buffer can provide peace of mind and allow for flexibility in your travels.

Currency Considerations: Panama uses the US dollar as its currency, which simplifies budgeting for many international travelers. However, be aware that some credit cards may charge foreign transaction fees, even though you're spending in dollars.

Crafting a budget for your Panama trip is more than just crunching numbers – it's about aligning your financial resources with your travel dreams. Whether you're watching your pennies as a budget traveler or splurging on luxury experiences, Panama's diverse offerings ensure that every type of traveler can create lasting memories. By planning ahead and understanding the costs associated with different aspects of your trip, you can focus on what really matters – immersing yourself in the beauty, culture, and adventures that Panama has to offer. Remember, the value of travel often lies in the experiences and connections you make, rather than the amount you spend. With thoughtful budgeting, your Panamanian adventure awaits, promising discovery, relaxation, and the joy of exploring one of Central America's most captivating destinations.

Chapter 2: Panama City: The Cosmopolitan Hub

Exploring the Old Town (Casco Viejo)

Stepping into Casco Viejo feels like traversing time itself. This historic district, perched on a peninsula jutting into the Pacific Ocean, stands in stark contrast to the soaring skyscrapers of modern Panama City. Casco Viejo, also known as Casco Antiguo or San Felipe, is a captivating blend of crumbling ruins and meticulously restored colonial buildings, where every cobblestone street whispers tales of pirates, prosperity, and perseverance.

Founded in 1673 after the destruction of the original Panama City (now known as Panama Viejo) by the infamous pirate Henry Morgan, Casco Viejo served as the heart of the city for centuries. Its strategic location, protected by defensive walls, helped safeguard the wealth flowing through Panama during the colonial era. Today, this UNESCO World Heritage site offers visitors a glimpse into Panama's rich history while pulsing with a vibrant, contemporary energy.

The architecture of Casco Viejo is a visual feast, showcasing a unique blend of Spanish colonial, French, and early American styles. Narrow streets lined with colorful buildings feature intricate balconies, often draped with cascading bougainvillea. The juxtaposition of meticulously restored structures alongside weathered, graffiti-adorned ruins creates a hauntingly beautiful urban landscape that begs to be photographed.

One of the most iconic spots in Casco Viejo is the Plaza de la Independencia, the main square where Panama declared its independence from Colombia in 1903. Dominated by the majestic Metropolitan Cathedral, whose pearly white towers took over 108 years to complete, this plaza buzzes with activity day and night. Street vendors sell traditional handicrafts, while locals and tourists alike gather on benches to people-watch and soak in the atmosphere.

Just a stone's throw from the plaza, the Iglesia de San José awaits, home to the famous Golden Altar. Legend has it that when pirate Henry Morgan sacked the original Panama City, a quick-thinking priest painted the solid gold altar black, convincing the pirates it was worthless. The altar was thus saved and later moved to its current home. Standing before this ornate masterpiece, gleaming with gold leaf, visitors can't help but feel a connection to Panama's tumultuous past.

For history buffs, the Panama History Museum, housed in the beautifully restored Municipal Palace, offers a deep dive into the country's rich heritage. From pre-Columbian artifacts to exhibits on the construction of the Panama Canal, the museum provides context to the sights and sounds experienced while wandering Casco Viejo's streets.

No visit to the old town is complete without a stroll along the Paseo Esteban Huertas. This promenade, built atop the old sea wall, offers breathtaking views of the Panama City skyline and the Bridge of the Americas spanning the Panama Canal entrance. The walkway is shaded by a canopy of bougainvillea, creating a romantic setting perfect for watching the sunset over the Pacific.

Casco Viejo's transformation in recent years has brought with it a flourishing culinary and nightlife scene. The American Trade Hotel, a lovingly restored landmark building, houses the Danilo's Jazz Club, where visitors can enjoy world-class jazz performances in an intimate setting. The hotel's Lobby Bar, with its colonial-inspired décor and craft cocktails, transports guests to another era.

For a taste of Panama's culinary heritage, Fonda Lo Que Hay offers a modern twist on traditional Panamanian dishes. Chef José Carles' innovative menu changes regularly, ensuring a unique dining experience with each visit. The restaurant's casual vibe and communal seating foster a sense of community among diners.

Coffee enthusiasts will find nirvana at Café Unido, where Panama's world-renowned geisha coffee takes center stage. Sipping a meticulously prepared pour-over while watching the world go by from the café's street-side seating is a quintessential Casco Viejo experience.

As night falls, the old town takes on a magical quality. Soft lighting illuminates the historic buildings, and the sounds of salsa music spill out from bustling bars. Tantalo Rooftop Bar offers panoramic views of the city skyline, serving up creative cocktails against a backdrop of twinkling lights. For a more laid-back evening, Casa Casco's multi-level venue provides options ranging from a casual pizzeria to a swanky rooftop lounge.

Art lovers will find plenty to admire in Casco Viejo. The area has become a haven for artists, with numerous galleries showcasing both local and international talents. Karavan Gallery, housed in a beautifully restored building, features rotating exhibitions of contemporary Panamanian art. Meanwhile, the vibrant street art adorning many of the area's crumbling buildings tells stories of social and political commentary.

Visitors seeking unique souvenirs will find Casco Viejo doesn't disappoint. Diablo Rosso, part art gallery, part concept store, offers a carefully curated selection of local designer goods and artwork. Meanwhile, the Karavan Eco-Concept Store focuses on sustainable and ethically produced items, from Panama hats (which, despite their name, originated in Ecuador) to handcrafted jewelry.

One of the most poignant spots in Casco Viejo is the Plaza de Francia, located at the tip of the peninsula. This square pays homage to the French influence in Panama, particularly their ill-fated attempt to build the Panama Canal. The plaza's centerpiece, an obelisk crowned with a Gallic rooster, is surrounded by plaques detailing the canal's history. From here, visitors can enjoy sweeping views of the Pacific Ocean and the modern city skyline, a striking visual representation of Panama's journey from colonial outpost to thriving metropolis.

While exploring Casco Viejo, take time to venture off the main tourist thoroughfares. In the quieter residential areas, you'll encounter locals going about their daily lives, children playing in small plazas, and the occasional stray cat sunning itself on a weathered doorstep. These moments offer a glimpse into the real life of the neighborhood, beyond the polished façade of the tourist areas.

The ongoing restoration of Casco Viejo is not without controversy. As the area gentrifies, long-time residents face the challenge of rising costs. However, efforts are being made to balance development with preservation of the community's character. The Fundación Calicanto, for instance, runs programs to help local residents benefit from the area's tourism boom through job training and education initiatives.

Whether you spend a few hours or a few days exploring Casco Viejo, the old town's charm is sure to leave a lasting impression. It's a place where every building tells a story, where the weight of history is palpable, yet the spirit of modern Panama shines through. From savoring a cup of world-class coffee in a centuries-old plaza to dancing the night away in a rooftop bar, Casco Viejo offers a multi-faceted experience that encapsulates the very essence of Panama – a country where past and present, tradition and innovation, coexist in captivating harmony.

Wandering the streets of this historic district transports you to another time. Imagine the colonial officials who once walked these same cobblestone streets, the revolutionaries who plotted independence, and the visionaries who saw potential in the crumbling ruins. Casco Viejo is more than just a tourist attraction; it's a living, breathing testament to Panama's resilience and creativity. It's a place that invites you to not just observe history, but to become a part of its ongoing story.

Modern Panama and Its Skyscrapers

Panama City's skyline is a testament to the country's rapid growth and modernization, a glittering array of architectural marvels that stand in stark contrast to the colonial charm of Casco Viejo. This juxtaposition of old and new creates a cityscape unlike any other in Central America, where centuries-old churches and ruins sit just a stone's throw from towering skyscrapers that pierce the tropical sky.

The transformation of Panama City from a modest urban center to a metropolis of gleaming glass and steel began in earnest in the 1990s, following the end of Manuel Noriega's regime and the subsequent economic boom. The handover of the Panama Canal from U.S. control in 1999 further accelerated this growth, with the city quickly becoming a hub for international business and finance in the region.

Today, the district of Punta Pacifica stands as the epitome of modern Panama. This man-made peninsula, jutting out into the Pacific Ocean, is home to some of the city's most impressive architectural achievements. The undisputed star of this skyline is the F&F Tower, more commonly known as El Tornillo (The Screw) due to its distinctive twisting design. This 52-story office building, completed in 2011, has become an iconic symbol of Panama's modernity and ambition.

Just a short distance away, the Trump Ocean Club International Hotel and Tower dominates the waterfront. Its sail-like shape, reminiscent of Dubai's Burj Al Arab, makes it instantly recognizable. At 70 stories, it held the title of tallest building in Latin America upon its completion in 2011, a crown it has since ceded but which speaks to Panama's architectural ambitions.

The banking district of Panama City, concentrated along Avenida Balboa and Calle 50, offers a canyon-like experience of towering financial institutions and corporate headquarters. The twin towers of BICSA Financial Center stand out with their sloping, knife-edge design, while the sail-shaped Banco Panama building adds a touch of nautical flair to the concrete jungle.

Perhaps the most ambitious project in modern Panama is Ocean Reef Islands, a pair of artificial islands under construction off the coast of Panama City. This development promises ultra-luxury residences with private marinas, showcasing Panama's continued push towards high-end real estate and exclusive living spaces.

The contrast between this hyper-modern cityscape and the historic districts is most striking from certain vantage points. Ancon Hill, the highest point within the city limits, offers panoramic views where one can simultaneously take in the colonial rooftops of Casco Viejo, the green expanse of the former Canal Zone, and the glittering towers of the banking district. This visual juxtaposition encapsulates Panama's journey from colonial outpost to 21st-century metropolis.

However, modern Panama isn't just about height and glamour. The city has also embraced innovative design in its public spaces and infrastructure. The Biomuseo, designed by world-renowned architect Frank Gehry, stands as a colorful landmark at the entrance to the Panama Canal. Its bold, fragmented design, inspired by the isthmus's natural and cultural history, provides a unique counterpoint to the sleek towers of the financial district.

The Panama Metro, Central America's first rapid transit system, represents another leap into modernity. Opened in 2014, the system now boasts two lines, with more planned. The clean, efficient stations and trains have transformed urban mobility in the capital, connecting disparate neighborhoods and reducing the city's notorious traffic congestion.

Another modern marvel is the Amador Causeway, a road connecting four small islands at the Pacific entrance to the Panama Canal. This area has been transformed into a leisure destination, with the addition of marinas, restaurants, and the striking Biodiversity Museum. The causeway offers unparalleled views of ships entering the canal, with the city skyline providing a dramatic backdrop.

While the rapid development has brought prosperity to many, it has also raised concerns about environmental impact and social inequality. The mangroves that once lined much of the city's coastline have largely been replaced by high-rises and marinas. Organizations like the Panama Audubon Society work to protect remaining green spaces and promote sustainable development.

The modernization of Panama City has also led to gentrification in some areas, most notably in Casco Viejo. As crumbling historic buildings are restored and converted into boutique hotels and upscale restaurants, long-time residents have faced rising costs and displacement. This has sparked ongoing debates about balancing progress with preservation of community and culture.

Despite these challenges, the overall sentiment in Panama remains optimistic about the country's modernization. The skyline serves as a point of national pride, a visible symbol of Panama's emergence as a major player in the global economy. This pride is palpable among locals, who often speak enthusiastically about the latest architectural projects and the city's growing international reputation.

For visitors, the modernity of Panama City often comes as a surprise. Many arrive expecting a typical Central American capital, only to find themselves in a city that can rival Miami or Singapore in terms of urban development. This unexpected modernity adds an exciting dimension to the travel experience, allowing visitors to enjoy world-class amenities alongside more traditional cultural attractions.

The city's modern face is perhaps best experienced after dark when the skyline transforms into a dazzling light show. Rooftop bars atop many of the high-rises offer the chance to take in these views while sipping craft cocktails. The Hard Rock Hotel's rooftop lounge and the aptly named Panaviera atop the Sortis Hotel are popular spots for both tourists and locals to marvel at the city's nocturnal beauty.

Architectural enthusiasts can explore the details of these modern marvels through "skyscraper tours" offered by several companies in the city. These tours provide insights into the design and construction of the most notable buildings, as well as the economic and cultural factors driving Panama's vertical growth.

It's worth noting that Panama's modernization extends beyond the capital. The beach town of Coronado, about an hour from Panama City, has seen its own high-rise boom, with luxury condominiums catering to both foreign retirees and wealthy Panamanians seeking weekend retreats. Even in more remote areas, evidence of Panama's economic growth can be seen in improved infrastructure and increasing access to technology.

Looking to the future, Panama shows no signs of slowing its modernization efforts. Plans are underway for even taller skyscrapers, more artificial islands, and continued expansion of public transportation. The Panama Canal's recent expansion has opened up new opportunities for growth, with the logistics and shipping sectors driving further development.

However, there's also a growing awareness of the need for sustainable development. Newer projects are incorporating green technologies and designs, with a focus on energy efficiency and reducing environmental impact. The planned Fourth Bridge over the Panama Canal, for instance, will not only ease traffic congestion but also incorporate lanes for the future expansion of the metro system.

Panama's embrace of modernity, as embodied by its impressive skyline, reflects a nation eager to define its place in the 21st century. It's a country that honors its past while boldly stepping into the future, creating a unique blend of experiences for both residents and visitors. From the colonial cobblestones of Casco Viejo to the soaring heights of Punta Pacifica, Panama offers a journey through time and progress, all within the span of a few city blocks.

For travelers, this juxtaposition provides a richly layered experience. One can start the day exploring historic sites, spend the afternoon shopping in world-class malls, and end the evening dining in a rooftop restaurant with panoramic views of the illuminated cityscape. It's this diversity, this seamless blending of old and new, that makes modern Panama such a fascinating destination.

Exploring the city offers opportunities to appreciate both the grandeur of the skyline and the small details of daily life unfolding in its shadow. In the end, it's not just the height of the buildings that impresses, but the spirit of ambition and optimism they represent – a spirit that infuses every aspect of life in this dynamic, ever-evolving country.

The Panama Canal: A Marvel of Engineering

The Panama Canal stands as a testament to human ingenuity and determination, transforming global maritime trade and capturing the imagination of travelers worldwide. This engineering masterpiece, slicing through the narrow isthmus of Panama, continues to awe visitors and shape international commerce over a century after its completion.

In 1881, the French embarked on an ambitious project to connect the Atlantic and Pacific Oceans. Led by Ferdinand de Lesseps, fresh from his success with the Suez Canal, the endeavor faced immense challenges. Tropical diseases, treacherous terrain, and financial mismanagement plagued the effort. By 1894, the French venture had collapsed, leaving behind a trail of failed dreams and lost lives.

The United States, recognizing the strategic and economic potential of a canal, took up the mantle in 1904. President Theodore Roosevelt, a driving force behind the project, negotiated control of the Canal Zone. The American effort, led by chief engineer John Frank Stevens and later George Washington Goethals, learned from French mistakes and implemented crucial changes.

They prioritized worker health, combating yellow fever and malaria under the guidance of Dr. William Gorgas. Innovative engineering solutions, including the design of a lock-based canal instead of a sea-level passage, proved pivotal. The Americans also harnessed the power of the Chagres River, creating Gatun Lake to aid ship transit.

After a decade of toil, involving over 75,000 workers from around the globe, the canal opened on August 15, 1914. The feat came at a tremendous cost - both in dollars and human lives. Thousands perished during construction, with the total death toll from both French and American efforts estimated at over 25,000.

Today, the Panama Canal serves as a vital artery of global trade, handling about 5% of the world's maritime commerce. Ships traversing the 50-mile waterway save nearly 8,000 miles compared to the perilous journey around Cape Horn. The canal operates 24/7, facilitating the passage of around 14,000 vessels annually.

The heart of the canal's function lies in its lock system. These enormous chambers act as water elevators, raising ships from sea level to the height of Gatun Lake, then lowering them back down on the other side. Each lock chamber requires about 52 million gallons of water to fill - a truly staggering amount.

In 2016, the canal underwent a significant expansion, adding a third set of locks to accommodate larger vessels. This $5.25 billion project allows the passage of "New Panamax" ships, capable of carrying up to 14,000 containers - nearly triple the previous capacity.

Visiting the Panama Canal offers a front-row seat to this marvel of human achievement. The Miraflores Visitor Center, just outside Panama City, provides an excellent vantage point to watch ships navigate the locks. Its museum offers insights into the canal's history, function, and ecological impact.

For a more immersive experience, travelers can book partial transits of the canal. These half-day journeys allow passengers to experience the lock system firsthand, rising and falling with the waters of Lake Gatun. The sensation of being lifted several stories in a massive ship is truly unforgettable.

Adventure seekers might opt for kayaking tours in Gatun Lake, paddling alongside mammoth cargo ships in the calm waters. This unique perspective highlights the contrast between human engineering and the lush rainforest that flanks the canal.

The Agua Clara Visitor Center, on the Atlantic side, offers views of the new expanded locks. Here, visitors can marvel at the immense scale of modern shipping, watching behemoths squeeze through with mere inches to spare.

Beyond its role in shipping, the canal has shaped Panama's ecosystems. Gatun Lake, once hilltops and valleys, now forms a unique freshwater habitat. Wildlife tours showcase howler monkeys, sloths, and a myriad of tropical birds that have adapted to this altered landscape.

The canal's impact extends far beyond its banks. It has been a catalyst for Panama's economic growth, contributing significantly to the country's GDP. The canal's influence is evident in Panama City's impressive skyline, a testament to the prosperity it has brought.

However, the canal faces challenges in the 21st century. Climate change threatens water levels in Gatun Lake, crucial for lock operations. Drought conditions in recent years have forced restrictions on ship drafts, impacting the canal's efficiency.

Moreover, alternative shipping routes loom on the horizon. The melting Arctic ice cap could open new pathways, while Nicaragua has long harbored ambitions for a competing canal. These potential changes underscore the need for continued innovation and adaptation in Panama.

Visiting the canal offers more than just an engineering spectacle. It's a journey through time, from the age of imperial ambitions to the globalized present. It's a story of human triumph over nature, but also a reminder of the ecological costs of progress.

The canal embodies the complexities of our modern world - the interplay of commerce, technology, and environment. It stands as a monument to human ambition and a harbinger of future challenges.

For travelers in 2024-2025, the Panama Canal remains an essential destination. It offers a unique blend of history, engineering marvel, and natural beauty. Whether watching from the visitor centers, transiting the locks, or exploring the surrounding rainforest, the canal provides unforgettable experiences.

The Panama Canal is more than a waterway - it's a window into the forces that shape our world. It continues to inspire awe, spark curiosity, and fuel dreams of what humans can achieve when they dare to reshape the very face of the Earth.

Top Museums and Cultural Sites

Panama City pulses with a vibrant cultural scene, offering visitors a rich tapestry of museums and historical sites that bring the country's diverse heritage to life. From pre-Columbian artifacts to cutting-edge contemporary art, these institutions provide captivating insights into Panama's past, present, and future.

Biomuseo

Perched at the entrance of the Panama Canal, this Frank Gehry-designed marvel is impossible to miss with its bold, colorful facade. The Biomuseo celebrates Panama's incredible biodiversity and its role as a land bridge between North and South America. Eight galleries explore the country's natural history, from its geological formation to its impact on global ecosystems.

Address: Amador Causeway, Building 136, Panama City
How to get there: Take a taxi or bus to the Amador Causeway. The museum is near the entrance.
Contact: +507 830-6700

Panama Viejo Museum and Visitor Center

Step back in time at the ruins of the original Panama City, founded in 1519 and destroyed by pirate Henry Morgan in 1671. The museum showcases artifacts from the colonial era and offers a glimpse into daily life in the first European settlement on the Pacific coast of the Americas.

Address: Vía Cincuentenario and Calle Domingo Díaz, Panama City
How to get there: A 15-minute drive from downtown. Taxis readily available.
Contact: +507 226-8915

Museo del Canal Interoceánico de Panamá

Housed in a beautifully restored 19th-century building, this museum tells the fascinating story of the Panama Canal. Exhibits cover everything from early Spanish colonial attempts to the modern canal's construction and operation.

Address: Plaza de la Independencia, Casco Viejo, Panama City
How to get there: Located in the heart of Casco Viejo, easily accessible on foot or by taxi.
Contact: +507 211-1649

Museo de Arte Contemporáneo (MAC Panama)

Panama's premier contemporary art museum showcases works by both established and emerging artists from

Panama and Latin America. The rotating exhibitions challenge perceptions and spark dialogue about current social issues.

Address: Calle San Blas, Ancón, Panama City
How to get there: A short taxi ride from downtown or Casco Viejo.
Contact: +507 262-8012

Museo Antropológico Reina Torres de Araúz

Named after a prominent Panamanian anthropologist, this museum houses an impressive collection of pre-Columbian artifacts. Visitors can explore the rich cultural heritage of Panama's indigenous peoples through ceramics, gold work, and traditional textiles.

Address: Calle Herbruger, Plaza 5 de Mayo, Panama City
How to get there: Located near the 5 de Mayo metro station.
Contact: +507 501-4000

Museo de la Mola

Dedicated to the intricate textile art of Panama's Guna people, this small museum offers a deep dive into the cultural significance and craftsmanship of molas. These colorful, layered fabric panels are an integral part of Guna identity and artistic expression.

Address: Calle 2da Oeste, Casco Viejo, Panama City
How to get there: Easily walkable within Casco Viejo.
Contact: +507 228-1747

Museo Afro-Antillano de Panamá

This museum celebrates the contributions of Afro-Caribbean immigrants who played a crucial role in building the Panama Canal. Exhibits highlight their cultural traditions, struggles, and lasting impact on Panamanian society.

Address: Calle 24 Este, Calidonia, Panama City
How to get there: A short taxi ride from downtown or accessible via the Metro (Lotería station).
Contact: +507 262-1668

Fundación Museo de Historia de Panamá

Housed in a lovingly restored colonial mansion, this museum offers a comprehensive overview of Panamanian history. From pre-Columbian times to the modern era, exhibits bring key moments and figures to life through artifacts, documents, and multimedia presentations.

Address: Calle 7a Este, Casco Viejo, Panama City
How to get there: Located in the heart of Casco Viejo, easily accessible on foot or by taxi.
Contact: +507 228-3825

Museo de la Biodiversidad y el Canal

This innovative museum combines natural history with canal engineering, showcasing Panama's unique ecosystems and their relationship to the waterway. Interactive exhibits allow visitors to explore the country's remarkable biodiversity.

Address: Calle 2a, Amador Causeway, Panama City
How to get there: Located on the Amador Causeway, accessible by taxi or bus.
Contact: +507 314-0097

Casa-Museo Banco Nacional de Panamá

Explore Panama's financial history in this beautifully preserved Art Deco building. The museum showcases the evolution of Panamanian currency and banking, with a particular focus on the country's economic development since independence.

Address: Avenida Central, between 2nd and 3rd Streets, Panama City
How to get there: Located in the city center, easily accessible by taxi or on foot from nearby hotels.
Contact: +507 394-2100

Museo de Historia de Panamá

This small but comprehensive museum offers a journey through Panama's history, from pre-Columbian times to the present day. Exhibits feature important historical documents, including the country's declaration of independence.

Address: Palacio Municipal, Casco Viejo, Panama City
How to get there: Centrally located in Casco Viejo, easily accessible on foot or by taxi.
Contact: +507 212-0338

Museo de Ciencias Naturales

Nature enthusiasts will appreciate this museum's extensive collection of Panamanian flora and fauna. Exhibits focus on the country's diverse ecosystems, from tropical rainforests to marine environments.

Address: Parque Natural Metropolitano, Panama City
How to get there: Located within the Metropolitan Natural Park, accessible by taxi or bus.
Contact: +507 232-5552

Each of these cultural institutions offers a unique window into Panama's rich heritage and contemporary culture. Visitors are encouraged to plan their itineraries to include a mix of these sites, allowing for a comprehensive understanding of the country's history, art, and natural wonders.

When visiting these museums and cultural sites, keep in mind that opening hours may vary, and some institutions may require advance booking, especially for guided tours.

It's always a good idea to check their websites or call ahead to confirm current information and any special exhibitions or events.

Many of these museums offer guided tours in multiple languages, providing deeper insights and context to the exhibits. Don't hesitate to ask about these options at the reception desk. Visitors with limited time can easily combine the museums in Casco Viejo (Panama's historic district) into a walking tour, allowing them to soak in the colonial architecture between museum visits.

Remember that Panama's cultural riches extend beyond the capital city. Regional museums and sites, such as the Museo de Herrera in Chitré or the Museo de Penonomé, offer fascinating glimpses into local history and traditions.

By exploring these top museums and cultural sites, visitors to Panama will gain a profound appreciation for the country's complex history, vibrant artistic scene, and incredible natural heritage. Each institution tells a unique part of Panama's story, inviting travelers to connect deeply with this diverse and dynamic nation.

Dining and Nightlife Scene

Panama City's dining and nightlife scene pulsates with energy, offering a tantalizing mix of flavors, sounds, and experiences that cater to every palate and preference. From world-class restaurants helmed by celebrity chefs to hidden local gems serving up authentic Panamanian fare, the city's culinary landscape is a gastronomic adventure waiting to be explored.

Let's start our journey through Panama City's vibrant food scene with some top-notch dining establishments:

Maito: Chef Mario Castrellón's flagship restaurant showcases Panama's diverse culinary heritage with a modern twist. The tasting menu is a revelation, featuring innovative dishes that incorporate indigenous ingredients and techniques.

- Address: Calle 50 Este, Panama City
- How to get there: Located in the Coco del Mar neighborhood, easily accessible by taxi
- Contact: +507 391-4657

- Rating: 4.7/5

Donde José: This intimate 16-seat restaurant offers a deep dive into Panamanian cuisine. Chef José Carles crafts an ever-changing menu that tells the story of Panama's culinary traditions and local ingredients.
- Address: Avenida Central, Casco Viejo, Panama City
- How to get there: Situated in the heart of Casco Viejo, walkable from most hotels in the area
- Contact: +507 262-1682
- Rating: 4.8/5

Restaurante Intimo: Chef Hernán Correa's cozy restaurant serves up creative, locally-sourced dishes in a warm, inviting atmosphere. The seasonal tasting menu is a culinary journey through Panama's diverse ecosystems.

- Address: Calle 50, Panama City
- How to get there: Located in the bustling financial district, easily reached by taxi
- Contact: +507 387-5441
- Rating: 4.6/5

Visitors seeking more budget-friendly options without compromising on flavor:

Mercado de Mariscos: This bustling fish market doubles as a food court, offering some of the freshest and most affordable seafood in the city. Don't miss the ceviche stands outside.

- Address: Avenida Balboa, Panama City
- How to get there: Located near Casco Viejo, accessible by foot or a short taxi ride
- Contact: No phone (open-air market)
- Rating: 4.4/5

El Trapiche: A Panama City institution, El Trapiche serves up hearty portions of traditional Panamanian fare. It's the perfect place to try local favorites like sancocho and carimañolas.

- Address: Vía Argentina, El Cangrejo, Panama City
- How to get there: Centrally located in El Cangrejo, easily reached by taxi or metro
- Contact: +507 269-4353
- Rating: 4.3/5

Now, let's dive into Panama City's pulsating nightlife scene:

Tantalo Rooftop Bar: Perched atop the stylish Tantalo Hotel in Casco Viejo, this rooftop bar offers breathtaking views of the city skyline. It's the perfect spot for sundowners and late-night cocktails.

- Address: Calle 8 Este con Avenida B, Casco Viejo, Panama City
- How to get there: Located in Casco Viejo, walkable from most hotels in the area
- Contact: +507 262-4030
- Rating: 4.5/5

La Rana Dorada: This craft brewery has several locations throughout the city, but the Casco Viejo branch is particularly charming. Sample their range of locally-brewed beers in a historic setting.

- Address: Avenida A, Casco Viejo, Panama City
- How to get there: Easily accessible on foot within Casco Viejo
- Contact: +507 212-2680
- Rating: 4.4/5

Casa Casco: This multi-level venue in Casco Viejo houses several bars and a rooftop with stunning views. Each floor offers a different vibe, from laid-back lounges to high-energy dance floors.

- Address: Avenida A, Casco Viejo, Panama City
- How to get there: Centrally located in Casco Viejo, walkable from nearby hotels
- Contact: +507 228-7613
- Rating: 4.3/5

People seeking an incredible time dancing:

Teatro Amador: Housed in a beautifully restored theater, this nightclub attracts a hip crowd with its eclectic mix of music genres and stunning visual projections.

- Address: Avenida Central, Casco Viejo, Panama City
- How to get there: Located in the heart of Casco Viejo, easily reached on foot or by taxi
- Contact: +507 211-2024
- Rating: 4.2/5

Panama's dining scene is characterized by its incredible diversity. The country's position as a crossroads of cultures is reflected in its cuisine, which blends indigenous, Spanish, African, and Caribbean influences.

In recent years, a new wave of chefs has been reimagining traditional Panamanian dishes, using local ingredients in innovative ways.

Seafood plays a starring role in many restaurants, thanks to Panama's access to both the Pacific Ocean and the Caribbean Sea. Ceviche, a dish of raw fish marinated in citrus juices, is a local specialty not to be missed. For meat lovers, the national dish of sancocho, a hearty chicken soup, is a must-try.

Panama's tropical climate means an abundance of fresh fruits and vegetables year-round. Many restaurants pride themselves on sourcing ingredients from local farms and markets, ensuring the freshest possible flavors.

The country's coffee culture is also worth exploring. Panama is home to some of the world's most expensive and sought-after coffee varieties, including the famed Geisha. Many cafes and restaurants offer cupping sessions and specialty brews that showcase the complexity of Panamanian coffee.

When it comes to nightlife, Panama City truly comes alive after dark. The historic neighborhood of Casco Viejo is the epicenter of the city's bar scene, with countless options ranging from craft cocktail bars to laid-back beer gardens. Many venues are housed in beautifully restored colonial buildings, adding a touch of history to your night out.

Rooftop bars have become increasingly popular in recent years, offering stunning views of the city skyline and the Panama Bay. These venues often feature live music or DJ sets, creating the perfect ambiance for a memorable evening.

Visitors craving a more high-energy experience will find Panama City boasting a number of world-class nightclubs. These venues often host international DJs and feature state-of-the-art sound and lighting systems. The dress code tends to be more formal at these establishments, so be sure to dress to impress.

Live music is also a big part of Panama's nightlife scene. From jazz clubs to salsa venues, there's something for every musical taste. Many bars and restaurants feature live performances, particularly on weekends, showcasing both local and international talent.

It's worth noting that Panama's nightlife tends to start late and go well into the early hours of the morning. Many locals don't head out until after 11 pm, and clubs often don't get busy until after midnight.

Safety is generally good in the main nightlife areas, but as with any big city, it's important to stay aware of your surroundings and use reputable taxi services when moving between venues.

Panama's drinking culture is vibrant and varied. While beer is popular, particularly local brands like Balboa and Atlas, there's also a growing craft beer scene. Rum is the spirit of choice for many Panamanians, with local brands like Ron Abuelo gaining international recognition.

In recent years, craft cocktail bars have been popping up across the city, offering creative concoctions that often incorporate local ingredients and spirits. These establishments are pushing the boundaries of mixology and providing a more sophisticated drinking experience.

Whether you're a foodie looking to explore new flavors, a night owl seeking the perfect dance floor, or simply someone who enjoys a good meal and a nice drink, Panama City's dining and nightlife scene has something to offer. The city's vibrant energy, diverse influences, and warm hospitality combine to create unforgettable experiences that will leave you wanting to come back for more.

Chapter 3: Beyond the Capital: Regions and Highlights

The Caribbean Coast

Panama's Caribbean coast unfolds like a dream, offering a stark contrast to the bustling energy of Panama City. Here, time seems to slow down, inviting visitors to lose themselves in pristine beaches, crystal-clear waters, and a laid-back atmosphere that embodies the essence of tropical paradise.

The region's character is shaped by its rich Afro-Caribbean heritage, evident in the vibrant music, spicy cuisine, and warm hospitality of its people. Colorful wooden houses line the streets of coastal towns, while reggae rhythms drift on the salty breeze. The Caribbean coast feels like a world apart, where nature reigns supreme and modern worries melt away under the warm sun.

One of the main attractions of Panama's Caribbean coast is the San Blas archipelago, a string of over 365 islands and cays that stretch along the coast. Home to the indigenous Guna people, San Blas offers a unique blend of natural beauty and cultural immersion. Visitors can island-hop on traditional dugout canoes, snorkel in crystal-clear waters teeming with marine life, and learn about Guna customs and traditions.

To experience San Blas, consider staying at:

Yandup Island Lodge: This eco-friendly resort offers overwater bungalows and beachfront cabins, providing an authentic Guna experience with modern comforts.

- Address: Playon Chico, Guna Yala, Panama
- How to get there: Fly from Panama City to Playon Chico, then take a short boat ride
- Contact: +507 6641-6668
- Rating: 4.7/5

Another jewel of the Caribbean coast is Bocas del Toro, an archipelago of islands that has become a hotspot for eco-tourism and marine adventures. Bocas Town, on Isla Colón, serves as the main hub, with its colorful Caribbean architecture and lively waterfront promenade. From here, visitors can explore the surrounding islands, each with its own unique charm.

Isla Bastimentos, part of the Bocas del Toro archipelago, is home to the stunning Red Frog Beach, named for the tiny strawberry poison dart frogs that inhabit the area. The island also encompasses a large part of Bastimentos National Marine Park, a protected area that's a haven for diverse marine life and nesting sea turtles.

For a luxurious stay in Bocas del Toro, consider:

Azul Paradise: This eco-luxury resort features overwater bungalows with private decks and direct access to the Caribbean Sea.

- Address: Isla Bastimentos, Bocas del Toro, Panama
- How to get there: Fly to Bocas del Toro, then take a boat to Isla Bastimentos
- Contact: +507 6592-4000
- Rating: 4.8/5

People seeking a more budget-friendly option:

Selina Bocas del Toro: This trendy hostel offers a variety of accommodations, from dorms to private rooms, with a lively social atmosphere.

- Address: Calle 3, Isla Colón, Bocas del Toro, Panama
- How to get there: Located in Bocas Town, easily accessible by foot or taxi from the airport
- Contact: +507 757-9081
- Rating: 4.3/5

Moving along the coast, the town of Portobelo offers a fascinating blend of history and natural beauty. Once the greatest Spanish port in Central America, Portobelo is now a sleepy fishing village surrounded by the ruins of colonial fortifications. The town's bay, with its calm turquoise waters, is perfect for kayaking and snorkeling.

For a unique stay in Portobelo:

El Otro Lado: This luxury retreat combines art, nature, and culture in a stunning waterfront setting.

- Address: Portobelo, Colón Province, Panama
- How to get there: Drive or take a bus from Panama City, then a short boat ride
- Contact: +507 202-0111
- Rating: 4.9/5

The Caribbean coast is a paradise for water sports enthusiasts. Surfing is popular in spots like Isla Colón and Isla Carenero in Bocas del Toro, with waves suitable for beginners and experienced surfers alike. Scuba diving and snorkeling opportunities abound, with vibrant coral reefs, sunken wrecks, and diverse marine life to explore.

People interested in learning to surf:

Mono Loco Surf School: Offers lessons for all levels and surf tours to the best spots around Bocas del Toro.

- Address: Isla Colón, Bocas del Toro, Panama
- How to get there: Located in Bocas Town, easily accessible on foot
- Contact: +507 6486-4655
- Rating: 4.8/5

The region's biodiversity extends beyond its marine environments. Lush rainforests teem with wildlife, offering opportunities for bird watching, hiking, and canopy tours. The Chagres National Park, which stretches from the Caribbean coast to the central highlands, is home to howler monkeys, sloths, and hundreds of bird species.

For an immersive rainforest experience:

Jungle Land Panama: This floating lodge in the Panama Canal watershed offers wildlife tours and kayaking adventures.

- Address: Gatun Lake, Colón Province, Panama
- How to get there: Pick-up from Panama City hotels available
- Contact: +507 6676-6563
- Rating: 4.9/5

The Caribbean coast's culinary scene is a reflection of its diverse cultural influences. Fresh seafood features prominently, often prepared with coconut milk and spices in traditional Afro-Caribbean style. Don't miss the chance to try rondon, a hearty seafood stew, or patacones, fried plantain discs that accompany many meals.

To sample authentic Caribbean cuisine:

Restaurante Dona Elma: This local favorite in Bocas Town serves up delicious Afro-Caribbean dishes in a casual setting.
- Address: Calle 3, Isla Colón, Bocas del Toro, Panama
- How to get there: Located in the heart of Bocas Town, easily walkable
- Contact: +507 757-9106
- Rating: 4.5/5

Getting to Panama's Caribbean coast typically involves flying or driving from Panama City. Bocas del Toro has its own airport with regular flights from the capital, while other destinations like Portobelo and Colón can be reached by car or bus. For San Blas, small planes fly to various airstrips in the comarca, followed by boat transfers to the islands.

When planning a trip to the Caribbean coast, it's important to consider the weather. The region experiences a tropical climate with high humidity and frequent rainfall, particularly from May to December. However, even during the rainy season, mornings are often sunny, with showers typically occurring in the afternoon.

Accommodations along the Caribbean coast range from luxurious eco-lodges to basic guesthouses. In popular areas like Bocas del Toro, options abound for every budget. In more remote locations like San Blas, lodging tends to be simpler, often in the form of basic cabins or even hammocks under thatched roofs.

To get a unique glamping experience:

Palmar Beach Lodge: This eco-friendly lodge offers safari-style tents and beachfront cabanas on a stunning stretch of coast.

- Address: Isla Colón, Bocas del Toro, Panama
- How to get there: Located on Bluff Beach, a short drive from Bocas Town
- Contact: +507 6572-8892
- Rating: 4.6/5

The Caribbean coast of Panama offers a rich tapestry of experiences, from adrenaline-pumping adventures to tranquil beach escapes. It's a place where you can disconnect from the outside world and reconnect with nature, where you can immerse yourself in vibrant cultures and create memories that will last a lifetime. Whether you're seeking relaxation, adventure, or cultural insights, Panama's Caribbean coast has something to offer every traveler.

The Pacific Coast

Panama's Pacific Coast stretches for over 1,000 kilometers, offering a diverse landscape of pristine beaches, rugged cliffs, and lush tropical forests. This region captivates visitors with its raw natural beauty, world-class surfing spots, and an array of eco-adventures. From bustling beach towns to secluded island getaways, the Pacific Coast provides a perfect blend of relaxation and excitement.

The character of Panama's Pacific Coast is one of contrasts. Near Panama City, you'll find developed beach communities and luxury resorts, while further down the coast, untouched beaches and small fishing villages offer a glimpse into a more tranquil way of life. The Pacific side is generally drier than the Caribbean coast, with a distinct dry season from December to April, making it ideal for sun-seekers and outdoor enthusiasts.

The Pearl Islands archipelago stands as a premier attraction along the Pacific Coast. This group of over 200 islands, made famous by the TV show "Survivor," offers pristine beaches, crystal-clear waters, and excellent opportunities for snorkeling and diving. The largest and most developed island, Contadora, serves as a base for exploring the archipelago.

Luxurious stay on Contadora Island:

The Point at Contadora Island: This boutique hotel offers stunning ocean views and a private beach.

- Address: Contadora Island, Pearl Islands, Panama
- How to get there: Take a ferry or short flight from Panama City
- Contact: +507 250-4200
- Rating: 4.7/5

Moving west from Panama City, the beach town of Coronado has become a popular weekend getaway for city dwellers and expats alike. Its long stretches of black and white sand beaches, golf courses, and modern amenities make it an attractive destination, offering a mix of relaxation and activities to visitors.

For a comfortable stay in Coronado:

Coronado Golf & Beach Resort: This resort offers spacious rooms, multiple pools, and access to a golf course.

- Address: Coronado Beach, Panama
- How to get there: About an hour's drive from Panama City
- Contact: +507 240-4444
- Rating: 4.4/5

Further down the coast, the Azuero Peninsula juts out into the Pacific, offering some of Panama's most beautiful and least crowded beaches. The town of Pedasi, on the peninsula's eastern coast, has gained popularity in recent years for its laid-back vibe and excellent surfing conditions.

For a boutique experience in Pedasi:

Villa Marina Lodge: This charming lodge offers comfortable rooms and easy access to nearby beaches.

- Address: Calle Panamericana, Pedasi, Los Santos, Panama
- How to get there: Drive or take a bus from Panama City (about 5 hours)
- Contact: +507 995-2324
- Rating: 4.6/5

Surfing is among the main draws of Panama's Pacific Coast, with world-class breaks scattered along its length. Santa Catalina, a small fishing village turned surf town, is renowned for its consistent waves and laid-back atmosphere. It's also the jumping-off point for trips to Coiba National Park, a UNESCO World Heritage site known for its pristine marine ecosystem.

Travelers interested in surfers and nature in Santa Catalina can try:

Hotel Santa Catalina: This eco-friendly hotel offers comfortable rooms and a prime location for surfing and diving trips.
- Address: Santa Catalina, Veraguas, Panama
- How to get there: Drive or take a bus from Panama City (about 6 hours)
- Contact: +507 6612-3001
- Rating: 4.5/5

The Gulf of Chiriqui, near the Costa Rican border, is home to some of Panama's most spectacular marine life. The Gulf of Chiriqui National Marine Park encompasses numerous islands and is a haven for whale watching, sport fishing, and snorkeling. Boca Chica serves as a gateway to this aquatic wonderland.

Getting a luxurious island retreat in the Gulf of Chiriqui:

Islas Secas Reserve & Lodge: This exclusive eco-resort offers private casitas on a stunning archipelago.

- Address: Islas Secas, Gulf of Chiriqui, Panama
- How to get there: Fly to David, then take a boat transfer
- Contact: +507 6776-2705
- Rating: 4.9/5

Beyond the beaches, the Pacific Coast offers a wealth of activities for nature lovers and adventure seekers. The

Cerro Hoya National Park, located on the southwestern tip of the Azuero Peninsula, stands as Panama's least explored regions. Its rugged terrain and diverse ecosystems make it a paradise for hikers and wildlife enthusiasts.

Eco-adventures near Cerro Hoya:

Eco Venao: This eco-lodge offers a range of accommodations and activities, from surfing to horseback riding.

- Address: Playa Venao, Los Santos, Panama
- How to get there: Drive or take a bus from Panama City (about 5 hours)
- Contact: +507 6677-8535
- Rating: 4.7/5

The Pacific Coast is also rich in cultural experiences. The town of Las Tablas, on the Azuero Peninsula, is famous for its Carnival celebrations, considered among the best in Panama. Throughout the year, various festivals and events showcase the region's folklore and traditions.

For a taste of local culture in Las Tablas:

Hotel Cañas: This conveniently situated motel provides cozy accommodations and quick access to neighborhood activities.

- Address: Calle 8 de Noviembre, Las Tablas, Los Santos, Panama
- How to get there: Drive or take a bus from Panama City (about 4 hours)
- Contact: +507 994-4144
- Rating: 4.2/5

Gastronomy along the Pacific Coast is a treat for seafood lovers. Fresh fish and shellfish feature prominently in local cuisine, often prepared with simple but flavorful techniques. Don't miss the chance to try corvina (sea bass) or langostinos (large prawns) at local restaurants.

Panga Restaurant: Located in Playa Venao, this beachfront restaurant offers fresh seafood and stunning ocean views.

- Address: Playa Venao, Los Santos, Panama
- How to get there: Located on Playa Venao beach
- Contact: +507 6982-1777
- Rating: 4.8/5

Getting to Panama's Pacific Coast destinations typically involves driving or taking a bus from Panama City. Some more remote locations, like Coiba National Park or the Pearl Islands, require boat transfers. For quicker access to distant spots like David (near Boca Chica), domestic flights are available from Panama City's Albrook Airport.

Accommodations along the Pacific Coast range from luxury resorts to eco-lodges and budget-friendly hostels. In more developed areas like Coronado and the Pearl Islands, you'll find high-end options with all the amenities. In smaller towns and more remote areas, lodgings tend to be simpler but often offer a more authentic experience.

For a unique glamping experience:

Eco Ventura Glamping: This eco-friendly site offers luxury tents with ocean views in Pedasi.

- Address: Playa El Toro, Pedasi, Los Santos, Panama
- How to get there: Drive or take a bus from Panama City, then a short drive from Pedasi town
- Contact: +507 6289-8492
- Rating: 4.6/5

When planning a trip to Panama's Pacific Coast, consider the seasonal variations. The dry season (December to April) is the most popular time to visit, with sunny weather perfect for beach activities. However, the green season (May to November) has its own charms, with lush landscapes and fewer crowds. Surfers might prefer to visit during the rainier months when swells are at their best.

The Pacific Coast of Panama offers a perfect blend of natural beauty, adventure, and relaxation. From world-class surfing and diving to tranquil beaches and rich cultural experiences, this region has something to offer every type of traveler. Whether you're seeking an adrenaline rush, a peaceful retreat, or a deep dive into local culture, Panama's Pacific Coast promises an unforgettable journey filled with diverse experiences and stunning landscapes.

Central Provinces

Panama's Central Provinces offer a captivating blend of natural wonders, rich cultural heritage, and off-the-beaten-path adventures. This diverse region, encompassing the provinces of Coclé, Herrera, Los Santos, and Veraguas, showcases Panama's heartland, where traditional rural life meets stunning landscapes and hidden gems awaiting discovery.

The character of the Central Provinces is deeply rooted in Panama's agricultural traditions. Rolling hills dotted with cattle ranches give way to verdant mountains, while pristine beaches line the coastline. Here, life moves at a slower pace, allowing visitors to immerse themselves in authentic Panamanian culture, from folklore festivals to artisanal crafts.

The region's star attraction is El Valle de Antón, a picturesque town nestled in the crater of an extinct volcano. Surrounded by lush cloud forests and blessed with a cool microclimate, El Valle is a haven for nature lovers and adventure seekers alike.

The Golden Frog Inn: This charming inn offers cozy rooms and beautiful gardens with mountain views.

- Address: Calle La Reforma, El Valle de Antón, Coclé, Panama

- How to get there: Two-hour drive from Panama City
- Contact: +507 983-6163
- Rating: 4.6/5

El Valle's natural wonders include the enigmatic square trees, found nowhere else in the world, and the picturesque Chorro El Macho waterfall. Visitors can hike through cloud forests, soak in hot springs, or explore the local market famous for its handicrafts and orchids.

For adventure enthusiasts:

Canopy Adventure El Valle: Offers thrilling zipline tours through the cloud forest canopy.

- Address: Near La India Dormida trail, El Valle de Antón, Coclé, Panama
- How to get there: Short drive or walk from El Valle town center
- Contact: +507 6676-7731
- Rating: 4.8/5

Moving towards the coast, the beaches of the Coclé province offer a more laid-back vibe compared to their Caribbean counterparts. Santa Clara and Farallon boast long stretches of golden sand, perfect for sunbathing, surfing, or simply unwinding.

For a beachfront stay:

Buenaventura Golf & Beach Resort: This luxurious resort offers world-class amenities and a stunning private beach.

Address: Riviera Pacifica, Río Hato, Coclé, Panama
How to get there: Two-hour drive from Panama City
Contact: +507 908-3333
Rating: 4.7/5

The province of Herrera is home to Chitré, often considered Panama's folklore capital. This charming town comes alive during the vibrant Carnival celebrations and the Festival Nacional de la Mejorana, showcasing traditional music, dance, and crafts.

Cultural immersion in Chitré:

Hotel Gran David: This conveniently situated hotel provides cozy accommodations and quick access to neighborhood activities.

- Address: Avenida Carmelo Spadafora, Chitré, Herrera, Panama
- How to get there: Four-hour drive from Panama City
- Contact: +507 996-2866
- Rating: 4.3/5

Near Chitré, the La Arena district is renowned for its clay artisans, producing beautiful pottery using pre-

Columbian techniques. Visitors may see artists at work and buy unique keepsakes.

The Los Santos province is the heart of Panama's cattle country and home to some of the nation's most cherished traditions. The town of Las Tablas hosts Panama's largest Carnival celebration, a riotous four-day festival of music, dance, and colorful parades.

To get a comfortable stay during Carnival:

Hotel Restaurante Las Tablas: This family-run hotel offers clean rooms and a central location perfect for enjoying the festivities.

- Address: Avenida Belisario Porras, Las Tablas, Los Santos, Panama
- How to get there: Four-hour drive from Panama City
- Contact: +507 994-4144
- Rating: 4.1/5

The Azuero Peninsula, shared by Los Santos and Herrera provinces, is known for its beautiful beaches and excellent surfing conditions. Playa Venao has become a popular spot for surfers of all levels.

For a surf-centric stay:

Eco Venao: This eco-lodge offers a range of accommodations from camping to private cabins, along with surf lessons and board rentals.

- Address: Playa Venao, Los Santos, Panama
- How to get there: Five-hour drive from Panama City
- Contact: +507 6677-8535
- Rating: 4.7/5

The province of Veraguas is a treasure trove of natural wonders. Santa Fe National Park offers spectacular hiking trails through cloud forests, pristine rivers, and waterfalls. The park is a paradise for birdwatchers, with over 300 species recorded.

For nature lovers visiting Santa Fe:

Hotel La Qhia: This eco-friendly hotel offers comfortable rooms and guided tours of the surrounding nature.

- Address: Santa Fe, Veraguas, Panama
- How to get there: Five-hour drive from Panama City
- Contact: +507 6570-2686
- Rating: 4.5/5

Santa Catalina, on the Veraguas coast, has gained fame as Panama's leading surfing destination. It's also the gateway to Coiba National Park, a UNESCO World Heritage site known for its rich marine life and pristine coral reefs.

For divers and surfers in Santa Catalina:

Hotel Santa Catalina: This laid-back hotel caters to surfers and divers with comfortable rooms and easy access to the beach.

- Address: Santa Catalina, Veraguas, Panama
- How to get there: Six-hour drive from Panama City
- Contact: +507 6612-3001
- Rating: 4.4/5

The Central Provinces offer a wealth of activities for outdoor enthusiasts. Hiking, birdwatching, and horseback riding are popular in the mountainous regions, while the coasts provide excellent opportunities for surfing, fishing, and whale watching (in season).

For a unique eco-adventure:

Canopy Lodge: Located in El Valle de Antón, this lodge specializes in birdwatching tours and nature walks.

- Address: El Valle de Antón, Coclé, Panama
- How to get there: Two-hour drive from Panama City
- Contact: +507 264-5720
- Rating: 4.9/5

The region's culinary scene is a reflection of its agricultural heritage. Fresh seafood, locally raised beef, and an abundance of tropical fruits feature prominently in local dishes. Don't miss the chance to try sancocho, a hearty chicken soup considered Panama's national dish.

To get a taste of local flavors:

Restaurante El Trapiche: This popular restaurant in Chitré serves traditional Panamanian dishes in a rustic setting.

- Address: Avenida Herrera, Chitré, Herrera, Panama
- How to get there: Located in downtown Chitré
- Contact: +507 996-4595
- Rating: 4.6/5

Getting to the Central Provinces typically involves driving from Panama City. The Pan-American Highway provides easy access to most major towns and attractions. For more remote destinations, local buses or guided tours may be necessary. Some areas, like Coiba National Park, require boat transfers.

Accommodations in the Central Provinces range from luxury beach resorts to rustic mountain lodges and small-town hotels. While you'll find high-end options in tourist hotspots, many areas offer a more authentic experience with family-run guesthouses and eco-lodges.

A unique stay:

Casa Mulata: This beautifully restored colonial house in Parita offers a glimpse into traditional Panamanian life.

- Address: Calle 5 de Noviembre, Parita, Herrera, Panama
- How to get there: Four-hour drive from Panama City
- Contact: +507 6273-8363
- Rating: 4.8/5

When planning a trip to Panama's Central Provinces, consider the seasonal variations. The dry season (December to April) is ideal for beach activities and outdoor adventures. However, the green season (May to November) brings lush landscapes and fewer crowds, perfect for exploring the region's natural beauty.

The Central Provinces of Panama offer a journey into the heart of Panamanian culture and nature. From cloud-forest hikes and world-class surfing to vibrant folklore festivals and tranquil beach retreats, this region provides a diverse array of experiences. Whether you're seeking adventure, cultural immersion, or simply a escape from the hustle and bustle of modern life, Panama's Central

Provinces promise an authentic and unforgettable experience.

Chiriquí Highlands

The Chiriquí Highlands, nestled in Panama's westernmost province, offer a refreshing escape from the tropical heat and a glimpse into a different side of Panama. This mountainous region, crowned by the dormant Volcán Barú, boasts a cool climate, misty cloud forests, and rolling hills covered in coffee plantations. The Highlands captivate visitors with their serene beauty, outdoor adventures, and charming mountain towns.

At the heart of the Chiriquí Highlands lies Boquete, a picturesque town that has become a haven for expats and eco-tourists alike. Surrounded by verdant mountains and blessed with a springlike climate year-round, Boquete serves as the perfect base for exploring the region's natural wonders.

Boquete's world-renowned coffee stands as a major attraction for visitors. The rich volcanic soil and ideal growing conditions produce some of the most sought-after coffee beans in the world, including the prized Geisha variety. Coffee enthusiasts can indulge in tours and tastings at local farms, learning about the intricate process from bean to cup.

An immersive coffee experience:

Finca Lérida Coffee Estate & Boutique Hotel: This historic coffee farm offers tours, tastings, and luxurious accommodations.

- Address: Alto Quiel, Boquete, Chiriquí, Panama
- How to get there: 15-minute drive from Boquete town center
- Contact: +507 720-1111
- Rating: 4.8/5

The natural beauty of the Chiriquí Highlands is best explored on foot. Numerous hiking trails crisscross the region, offering everything from leisurely walks to challenging treks. The crown jewel of hiking in the area is the ascent of Volcán Barú, Panama's highest peak. Intrepid hikers who make the overnight climb are rewarded with breathtaking views of both the Pacific Ocean and the Caribbean Sea on clear mornings.

Guided hiking adventures:

Boquete Outdoor Adventures: Offers a range of tours including the Volcán Barú trek and waterfall hikes.

- Address: Central Park, Boquete, Chiriquí, Panama
- How to get there: Located in downtown Boquete
- Contact: +507 6631-0163
- Rating: 4.9/5

The Chiriquí Highlands are a paradise for birdwatchers, with over 500 species recorded in the area. The elusive Resplendent Quetzal, with its vibrant plumage, is a top prize for many birders. The best spot for quetzal sightings is the Los Quetzales Trail in Volcán Barú National Park.

Serious birders take note:

Mount Totumas Cloud Forest: This private reserve offers guided birding tours and eco-friendly accommodations.

- Address: Cerro Punta, Chiriquí, Panama
- How to get there: 1-hour drive from Boquete
- Contact: +507 6950-7950
- Rating: 4.7/5

Adrenaline seekers will find plenty to keep them occupied in the Highlands. White water rafting on the Chiriquí Viejo River offers thrills for all skill levels, with Class II to Class V rapids depending on the section and season.

For rafting adventures:

Chiriqui River Rafting: Provides professional guides and equipment for rafting trips.

- Address: Av Central, Boquete, Chiriquí, Panama
- How to get there: Located in downtown Boquete
- Contact: +507 6613-0934
- Rating: 4.8/5

The charming town of Cerro Punta, nestled in a valley at the foot of Volcán Barú, is known for its agricultural prowess. The town supplies much of Panama with fresh produce, thanks to its cool climate and fertile soil. Visitors can tour strawberry farms, sample local products, and enjoy the bucolic scenery.

A farm stay experience:

Cielito Sur Bed & Breakfast: This cozy B&B offers comfortable rooms and beautiful gardens.

- Address: Guadalupe, Cerro Punta, Chiriquí, Panama
- How to get there: 45-minute drive from Boquete
- Contact: +507 6571-5327
- Rating: 4.6/5

The Chiriquí Highlands are also home to Panama's only tea plantation. The Kotowa Tea Estate in Boquete offers tours where visitors can learn about tea production and sample various blends.

For tea lovers:

Kotowa Coffee & Tea House: Offers tea tastings and a cafe with panoramic views.

Address: Alto Boquete, Boquete, Chiriquí, Panama

How to get there: 10-minute drive from Boquete town center
Contact: +507 720-3852
Rating: 4.5/5

Adventure seekers can get their adrenaline fix with zip-lining tours through the cloud forest canopy. These tours offer a unique perspective on the lush ecosystem and stunning views of the surrounding mountains.

Zip-lining thrills:

Tree Trek Boquete: Offers canopy tours with multiple zip-lines and hanging bridges.

- Address: Alto Boquete, Boquete, Chiriquí, Panama
- How to get there: 15-minute drive from Boquete town center
- Contact: +507 6949-8789
- Rating: 4.7/5

The Chiriquí Highlands are also known for their therapeutic hot springs. The Caldera Hot Springs, just outside Boquete, offer a relaxing soak in mineral-rich waters surrounded by lush vegetation.

For a relaxing retreat:

Refugio del Río: This riverside lodge offers access to natural hot springs and comfortable accommodations.

- Address: Caldera, Boquete, Chiriquí, Panama
- How to get there: 30-minute drive from Boquete
- Contact: +507 6612-2147
- Rating: 4.4/5

The culinary scene in the Chiriquí Highlands is a delightful mix of traditional Panamanian fare and international cuisine, often featuring locally grown produce and trout from mountain streams. The cool climate also allows for the cultivation of strawberries, blackberries, and other fruits not commonly found in tropical Panama.

A farm-to-table dining experience:

The Rock: This upscale restaurant in Boquete offers innovative dishes using local ingredients.

- Address: Calle 7 Sur, Boquete, Chiriquí, Panama
- How to get there: Located in downtown Boquete
- Contact: +507 6679-4525
- Rating: 4.8/5

Getting to the Chiriquí Highlands typically involves flying to David, the capital of Chiriquí province, from Panama City. From David, it's about a 45-minute drive to Boquete. Alternatively, buses run regularly from Panama City to David and then on to Boquete. Travelers with ample time can enjoy the drive from Panama City to Boquete, which takes about 7 hours and offers beautiful scenery along with opportunities to explore points of interest en route.

Accommodations in the Chiriquí Highlands range from luxurious spa resorts to cozy bed and breakfasts and eco-lodges. Many offer stunning mountain views and lush gardens.

luxury stay:

Valle Escondido Resort Golf & Spa: This upscale resort offers a golf course, spa, and multiple dining options.

- Address: Valle Escondido, Boquete, Chiriquí, Panama
- How to get there: 5-minute drive from Boquete town center
- Contact: +507 720-2200
- Rating: 4.6/5

For budget travelers:

Mamallena Hostel: In a prime downtown location, this welcoming hostel provides both shared and private rooms.

- Address: Av Central, Boquete, Chiriquí, Panama
- How to get there: Located in downtown Boquete
- Contact: +507 720-1260
- Rating: 4.3/5

When planning a trip to the Chiriquí Highlands, keep in mind that the region has a unique microclimate. While it's generally cooler than the rest of Panama, temperatures can still vary significantly between day and night. The dry season (December to April) offers the best weather for outdoor activities, but the green season (May to November) brings lush landscapes and fewer crowds.

The Chiriquí Highlands offer a refreshing contrast to Panama's tropical coasts and bustling capital. With its cool climate, stunning natural beauty, and wealth of outdoor activities, this region provides a perfect retreat for nature lovers, adventure seekers, and those simply looking to escape the heat. Whether you're sipping world-class coffee with a view of misty mountains, hiking through cloud forests in search of rare birds, or soaking in natural hot springs, the Chiriquí Highlands promise an unforgettable Panamanian highland experience.

San Blas Islands and Guna Yala

The San Blas Islands and Guna Yala region of Panama offer a glimpse into a world seemingly untouched by time, where pristine beaches meet turquoise waters and indigenous culture thrives. This archipelago of over 365 islands, stretching along Panama's Caribbean coast, is an autonomous territory governed by the Guna people, who have maintained their traditional way of life for centuries.

The character of San Blas and Guna Yala is defined by its stunning natural beauty and rich cultural heritage. Picture-perfect islands, many no larger than a football field, are fringed by powder-white sand and swaying coconut palms. The surrounding waters teem with vibrant coral reefs, offering a paradise for snorkelers and marine life enthusiasts.

What sets this region apart is the strong presence of Guna culture. The Guna people, known for their colorful mola textiles and fiercely independent spirit, welcome visitors while carefully preserving their traditions and environment. This unique blend of natural wonders and living culture creates an unforgettable experience for travelers seeking authenticity and connection.

Island hopping stands out as a primary attraction in San Blas. With hundreds of islands to choose from, each day can bring a new tropical paradise to explore. Many tours offer visits to multiple islands, allowing visitors to experience the diversity of the archipelago.

For a culturally immersive island-hopping experience:

San Blas Adventures: Offers multi-day tours that combine island visits with cultural interactions.

- Contact: +507 6677-0482
- Rating: 4.8/5
- Note: Tours depart from Carti, accessible by 4x4 from Panama City

The crystal-clear waters surrounding the islands are perfect for snorkeling and diving. Vibrant coral reefs host a diverse array of marine life, from colorful tropical fish to graceful sea turtles. Some areas also feature shipwrecks, adding an element of underwater adventure.

For snorkeling and diving excursions:

Panama Dive Center: Provides professional diving instruction and guided snorkeling tours.

- Address: Based in Panama City with trips to San Blas
- Contact: +507 6998-8807
- Rating: 4.7/5

Visiting a Guna village stands out as a particularly enriching experience in Guna Yala. These communities offer insight into traditional Guna life, from thatched-roof huts to the intricate process of mola-making. Respectful visitors are often welcomed to observe daily activities and purchase handmade crafts directly from artisans.

For cultural tours:

Guna Yala Cultural Experience: Offers guided visits to Guna communities with local Guna guides.

- Contact: +507 6747-0589
- Rating: 4.6/5
- Note: Tours arranged through accommodations on various islands

The region's main hub is the island of El Porvenir, which houses the airport and administrative offices. While not a typical tourist destination, it serves as a gateway to the smaller, more idyllic islands.

For a comfortable stay near the hub:

Hotel Wailidup: Offers overwater bungalows and easy access to multiple islands.

- Address: Isla Wailidup, Guna Yala, Panama
- Contact: +507 6189-6104
- Rating: 4.5/5

Travelers desiring a more remote experience will find the island of Isla Diablo to be a perfect escape. Known for its pristine beaches and excellent snorkeling, it provides a true desert island feel.

For a secluded island retreat:

Yandup Island Lodge: Eco-friendly cabins with traditional Guna architecture and modern comforts.

- Address: Playon Chico, Guna Yala, Panama
- Contact: +507 6641-6668
- Rating: 4.7/5

Sailing enthusiasts can explore the archipelago on multi-day catamaran trips. These journeys offer the chance to visit more remote islands and enjoy activities like kayaking and paddleboarding.

For sailing adventures:

San Blas Sailing: Offers multi-day catamaran trips with experienced captains.

- Contact: +507 6590-8800
- Rating: 4.9/5
- Note: Trips depart from Puerto Lindo, a 2-hour drive from Panama City

Fishing is an integral part of Guna life, and visitors can join local fishermen for traditional spearfishing expeditions. These trips not only provide an exciting activity but also offer insight into sustainable fishing practices that have sustained the Guna for generations.

For traditional fishing experiences:

Guna Fishing Adventures: Arranges spearfishing trips with local Guna guides.

- Contact: +507 6855-3421
- Rating: 4.6/5
- Note: Trips arranged through accommodations on various islands

The cuisine of Guna Yala reflects its coastal location, with fresh seafood featuring prominently. Lobster, crab, and various fish are often prepared simply, allowing their natural flavors to shine. Coconut is another staple, used in many dishes and drinks.

For a taste of local flavors:

Akwadup Lodge Restaurant: Serves traditional Guna dishes with a focus on fresh seafood.
- Address: Isla Akwadup, Guna Yala, Panama
- Contact: +507 6879-3745
- Rating: 4.4/5

Accommodations in San Blas and Guna Yala range from basic cabanas to more comfortable eco-lodges. Many are built in traditional Guna style with modern amenities. It's important to note that even the more upscale options are relatively rustic compared to mainland resorts, reflecting the region's commitment to environmental preservation.

For a mix of comfort and authenticity:

Akwadup Lodge: Offers overwater bungalows with solar power and eco-friendly practices.

- Address: Isla Akwadup, Guna Yala, Panama
- Contact: +507 6879-3745
- Rating: 4.6/5

For budget travelers:

Cabañas Ogob Nega: Basic but clean accommodations run by a Guna family.

- Address: Isla Ogob Nega, Guna Yala, Panama
- Contact: +507 6559-9697
- Rating: 4.2/5

Getting to San Blas and Guna Yala requires some planning. The most common route is to fly from Panama City to El Porvenir, then take a boat to your final island destination. Alternatively, 4x4 vehicles can make the journey from Panama City to the port of Carti, followed by a boat transfer. It's crucial to arrange transportation and accommodations in advance, as options are limited and often book up quickly.

When planning a trip to San Blas and Guna Yala, it's essential to respect local customs and environmental regulations. The Guna have strict rules to preserve their culture and ecosystem, including limitations on photography in some areas and restrictions on removing natural objects from the islands.

The best time to visit is during the dry season from December to April, when rainfall is minimal and seas are calmer. However, the region's tropical climate means brief showers can occur year-round.

Visitors should be prepared for a digital detox, as internet access is limited or non-existent on many islands. This disconnection from the outside world allows for a deeper immersion in the natural beauty and cultural richness of the region.

San Blas and Guna Yala offer a rare opportunity to experience a pristine tropical paradise while engaging with a living indigenous culture. The simplicity of life on the islands, coupled with breathtaking natural beauty, creates a profound sense of peace and connection with nature.

Whether you're lounging on a deserted beach, snorkeling among colorful fish, learning traditional crafts from Guna artisans, or simply swaying in a hammock with a coconut in hand, the San Blas Islands and Guna Yala provide an escape from the modern world and a chance to experience the raw beauty of Panama's Caribbean coast.

This unique destination challenges visitors to slow down, appreciate the simple pleasures of island life, and gain a deeper understanding of a culture that has maintained its traditions in the face of globalization. A journey to San Blas and Guna Yala is more than a vacation; It's an opportunity for personal growth, cultural exchange, and unforgettable memories in a rare unspoiled paradise.

Chapter 4: Adventures in Nature

National Parks and Wildlife Reserves

Panama's national parks and wildlife reserves showcase the country's incredible biodiversity, offering visitors the chance to explore pristine ecosystems teeming with exotic flora and fauna. From misty cloud forests to coral-rich marine parks, these protected areas provide unforgettable encounters with nature and a deeper appreciation for Panama's conservation efforts.

Soberanía National Park

Just a short drive from Panama City, Soberanía National Park offers visitors a taste of tropical rainforest teeming with wildlife.

Address: Panama Province, Panama
How to get there: 45-minute drive from Panama City. Accessible by car or organized tour.

Unique features:

- Over 525 bird species recorded within the park
- Famous Pipeline Road, a top global birding destination
- Diverse tropical rainforest ecosystems

Wildlife spotting opportunities:

- Toucans, trogons, and the elusive harpy eagle
- Howler monkeys, sloths, and white-faced capuchins
- Jaguars and ocelots (rarely seen)

Soberanía's proximity to Panama City makes it an ideal day trip for nature lovers. The park's Pipeline Road is legendary among birders, offering the chance to spot hundreds of species in a single day. Early morning visits increase the likelihood of wildlife encounters, as animals are most active during the cooler hours. Guided tours can greatly enhance the experience, with knowledgeable naturalists pointing out easily missed creatures hiding in the dense foliage.

Volcán Barú National Park

Home to Panama's only volcano and highest peak, Volcán Barú National Park offers stunning vistas and unique high-altitude ecosystems.

Address: Chiriquí Province, Panama
How to get there: Fly to David, then drive or take a bus to Boquete (1 hour). The park entrance is a short drive from Boquete.

Unique features:

- Panama's highest point at 3,475 meters (11,401 feet)
- Views of both the Pacific Ocean and Caribbean Sea on clear days
- Cloud forests with unique flora and fauna

Wildlife spotting opportunities:

- Resplendent quetzals (best seen from February to May)
- Over 250 bird species
- Pumas and Baird's tapirs (rarely seen)

The challenging hike to the summit of Volcán Barú rewards adventurers with breathtaking views and the rare opportunity to see both of Panama's coastlines simultaneously. The park's cloud forests are home to the elusive resplendent quetzal, widely regarded as among the world's most beautiful birds. The best time to spot quetzals is during their breeding season from February to May.

Chagres National Park

Protecting the watershed that feeds the Panama Canal, Chagres National Park offers a mix of rainforest adventures and cultural experiences with indigenous communities.

Address: Panama Province, Panama
How to get there: 90-minute drive from Panama City. Accessible by car or organized tour.

Unique features:

- Source of 40% of the water used in the Panama Canal
- Home to Emberá indigenous communities

- Diverse ecosystems from lowland rainforest to cloud forest

Wildlife spotting opportunities:

- Toucans, parrots, and various raptor species
- White-faced capuchin and howler monkeys
- Jaguars and pumas (rarely seen)

Chagres offers visitors the unique opportunity to combine wildlife watching with cultural immersion. Guided tours often include visits to Emberá villages, where visitors can learn about traditional ways of life and even participate in activities like medicinal plant walks. The park's rivers provide excellent opportunities for wildlife spotting, with boat trips offering chances to see animals coming to the water's edge.

Bastimentos Island National Marine Park

Located in the Bocas del Toro archipelago, this marine park protects coral reefs, mangrove forests, and nesting beaches for sea turtles.

Address: Bocas del Toro Province, Panama
How to get there: Fly to Bocas del Toro from Panama City, then take a water taxi to Bastimentos Island.

Unique features:

- Panama's first marine park

- Diverse ecosystems including coral reefs, mangroves, and rainforests
- Important nesting sites for sea turtles

Wildlife spotting opportunities:

- Four species of sea turtles
- Sloths and various monkey species
- Red-eyed tree frogs and strawberry poison dart frogs
- Diverse marine life including dolphins and nurse sharks

Bastimentos offers a perfect blend of terrestrial and marine ecosystems. Snorkeling and diving trips reveal vibrant coral reefs teeming with tropical fish, while hikes through the island's interior might lead to encounters with sloths lazily munching leaves or tiny, brightly colored poison dart frogs hopping along the forest floor. During nesting season, visitors can witness the incredible sight of sea turtles laying their eggs on moonlit beaches.

La Amistad International Park

Straddling the border between Panama and Costa Rica, La Amistad is a vast protected area known for its exceptional biodiversity.

Address: Chiriquí and Bocas del Toro Provinces, Panama

How to get there: Fly to David, then drive to the town of Cerro Punta (2 hours). Access to the park is via guided tours from Cerro Punta.

Unique features:

- UNESCO World Heritage site
- A notably large and exceptionally diverse natural area in Central America
- Home to a wide variety of species that are unique to this region

Wildlife spotting opportunities:

- Over 600 bird species, including the resplendent quetzal
- All six species of wild cats found in Central America
- Baird's tapirs and giant anteaters
- Thousands of plant species, including many orchids

La Amistad's remote location and rugged terrain have helped preserve its pristine ecosystems. Visitors willing to venture into its depths are rewarded with glimpses of some of Central America's most elusive wildlife. The park's high-altitude cloud forests are home to an incredible diversity of orchids, with new species still being discovered.

These national parks and wildlife reserves offer visitors the chance to experience Panama's natural wonders up close. From the depths of coral reefs to the heights of misty mountain peaks, each protected area tells a unique story of biodiversity and conservation. Whether you're an avid birder, a wildlife photographer, or simply a nature lover seeking connection with the wild, Panama's parks provide endless opportunities for discovery and adventure.

Hiking and Birdwatching

Panama's diverse landscapes offer a paradise for hiking enthusiasts and birdwatchers alike. From misty cloud forests to tropical lowlands, the country's varied ecosystems provide endless opportunities for outdoor adventures and wildlife encounters. Lace up your boots and grab your binoculars – Panama's natural wonders await.

Top Hiking Trails:

1. Sendero Los Quetzales

Location: Volcán Barú National Park, Chiriquí Province
Difficulty: Moderate to Challenging
Length: 9.6 km (6 miles) one-way

How to get there: Fly to David, then take a bus or drive to Boquete. The trail starts in Boquete and ends in Cerro Punta (or vice versa).

This iconic trail winds through the cloud forests of Volcán Barú, offering breathtaking views and the chance to spot the resplendent quetzal. The path meanders through lush vegetation, crossing streams and revealing stunning vistas of the surrounding mountains. The varying elevations make this hike challenging, but the rewards are well worth the effort. Keep an eye out for orchids, bromeliads, and a variety of bird species along the way.

2. La Amistad International Park Trails

Location: Chiriquí Province
Difficulty: Moderate to Challenging
Length: Various trails, ranging from 5 km to multi-day treks

How to get there: Fly to David, then drive to the town of Cerro Punta. Access to the park is via guided tours from Cerro Punta.

La Amistad offers several trails through pristine cloud forests and páramo ecosystems. The Las Nubes Trail is popular for day hikes, while longer routes like the Sendero La Cascada offer more challenging multi-day experiences. These trails provide opportunities to see rare birds, orchids, and if you're lucky, elusive mammals like tapirs.

3. Metropolitan Natural Park Trails

Location: Panama City
Difficulty: Easy
Length: Various trails, ranging from 1.2 km to 2.5 km

How to get there: Located within Panama City, easily accessible by taxi or bus.

For a quick nature escape within the city, the Metropolitan Natural Park offers several short trails through tropical dry forest. The Mono Tití trail is excellent for spotting Geoffrey's tamarins, while the Cieneguita trail leads to a scenic lookout over Panama City. These trails provide a perfect introduction to Panama's flora and fauna for beginners or those short on time.

Top Birdwatching Locations:

1. Pipeline Road, Soberanía National Park

Species to spot: Toucans, trogons, motmots, antbirds, and with luck, the elusive harpy eagle
How to get there: 45-minute drive from Panama City to Gamboa, then a short drive to the Rainforest Discovery Center

Renowned globally, Pipeline Road has recorded over 500 bird species. The Rainforest Discovery Center's 32-meter observation tower offers panoramic views of the canopy, perfect for spotting canopy-dwelling species. Early morning visits are best, when bird activity is at its peak.

2. El Valle de Antón

Species to spot: Toucans, parrots, hummingbirds, and the sought-after orange-bellied trogon

How to get there: Two-hour drive from Panama City

This picturesque town, set in the crater of an extinct volcano, offers excellent birding opportunities. The Canopy Lodge area and the trails of Cerro Gaital Natural Monument are particularly productive. The diverse habitats, from cloud forest to dry forest, support a wide variety of bird species.

3. Cerro Punta, Chiriquí Highlands

Species to spot: Resplendent quetzal, black-and-yellow silky flycatcher, long-tailed silky flycatcher

How to get there: Fly to David, then drive 1.5 hours to Cerro Punta

The highlands around Cerro Punta offer some of Panama's best cloud forest birding. The Respingo Trail and the roads around Volcán are excellent spots. The area is particularly famous for quetzal sightings, especially during their breeding season from February to May.

4. San San Pond Sak Wetlands

Species to spot: Waterfowl, herons, kingfishers, and migratory shorebirds

How to get there: Located near Changuinola in Bocas del Toro Province. Fly to Bocas del Toro, then arrange transportation to the wetlands.

These extensive wetlands provide crucial habitat for both resident and migratory birds. Boat tours through the mangrove channels offer excellent birding opportunities. The area is also important for manatees and sea turtles, adding to its wildlife appeal.

5. Darién National Park

Species to spot: Harpy eagle, great green macaw, black-tipped cotinga, and numerous other rare species
How to get there: Fly to Panama City, then take a domestic flight to El Real. Guided tours are essential for visiting this remote area.

Darién offers some of the most exciting, if challenging, birding in Panama. The chance to see harpy eagles in the wild draws many birders to this remote region. The park's vast wilderness harbors many species difficult or impossible to see elsewhere in Central America.

6. Achiote Road, Colón Province

Species to spot: Spot-crowned barbet, black-breasted puffbird, blue cotinga
How to get there: Two-hour drive from Panama City

This accessible road on the Caribbean slope offers excellent birding without the need for strenuous hiking. The road passes through a variety of habitats, including forest edges and wetlands, supporting a diverse bird community.

7. Cerro Azul

Species to spot: Violet-capped hummingbird, stripe-cheeked woodpecker, tacarcuna bush tanager
How to get there: One-hour drive from Panama City

The forests of Cerro Azul, at higher elevations than nearby Panama City, host several species not found in the lowlands. The community is private, so hiring a local guide is recommended for access to the best birding spots.

Whether you're an avid hiker seeking challenging trails or a passionate birder in search of rare species, Panama offers a wealth of opportunities. The country's commitment to preserving its natural heritage means that many of these areas remain pristine, providing authentic wilderness experiences.

When planning hiking and birdwatching excursions, consider the following tips:

- The best time for birdwatching is typically early morning or late afternoon when birds are most active.
- Hire local guides when possible. They possess invaluable knowledge about trail conditions and wildlife behavior.
- Be prepared for sudden weather changes, especially in mountain and cloud forest areas.

- Respect wildlife and follow Leave No Trace principles to help preserve these beautiful environments for future generations.

Panama's trails and birding hotspots offer more than just physical activity or species checklists – they provide windows into the country's incredible biodiversity and opportunities for profound connections with nature. Whether you're standing in awe of a resplendent quetzal in the misty cloud forests of Chiriquí or marveling at the cacophony of life in a lowland rainforest, these experiences will leave you with lasting memories and a deeper appreciation for Panama's natural wonders.

Water Sports and Beach Activities

Panama's coastlines are a playground for water enthusiasts and beach lovers. From the Caribbean's turquoise waters to the Pacific's powerful waves, this Central American gem offers a diverse array of aquatic adventures and sun-soaked relaxation spots. Let's dive into the exciting world of water sports and beach activities that await visitors to Panama in 2024-2025.

Surfing reigns supreme along Panama's Pacific coast. Playa Venao, a crescent-shaped beach in the Azuero Peninsula, draws surfers from around the globe with its consistent waves and laid-back vibe. Beginners can catch their first rides here, while seasoned surfers challenge themselves on the more demanding breaks. The nearby town caters to the surfing crowd with board rentals, lessons, and beachfront accommodations.

Surfers craving a more secluded experience will find Santa Catalina beckoning. This remote fishing village has transformed into a surf mecca, offering world-class waves at Punta Roca. The long, powerful right-hand point break tests even the most skilled surfers. Between sessions, visitors can explore the lush surroundings or take a boat trip to Coiba National Park, a UNESCO World Heritage site teeming with marine life.

Speaking of marine life, Panama's waters are a treasure trove for snorkeling and scuba diving enthusiasts. The Bocas del Toro archipelago in the Caribbean Sea is a paradise of coral reefs, shipwrecks, and vibrant underwater ecosystems. Isla Bastimentos National Marine Park protects a vast area of mangroves, coral reefs, and nesting sites for sea turtles. Divers can explore the Crawl Cay reef system, home to colorful fish, rays, and the occasional nurse shark.

For a truly unique diving experience, head to Portobelo on the Caribbean coast. This historic town, once a bustling Spanish colonial port, offers wreck diving opportunities among centuries-old galleons. Imagine swimming through the remnants of maritime history, surrounded by schools of tropical fish and encrusted coral formations.

Thrill-seekers will find their adrenaline fix with kitesurfing and windsurfing in Punta Chame. This narrow peninsula jutting into the Pacific Ocean benefits from steady winds and flat waters, creating ideal conditions for these high-octane sports. Numerous schools offer lessons and equipment rentals, making it accessible for beginners to experience the rush of harnessing the wind's power.

For a more relaxed pace, kayaking and stand-up paddleboarding (SUP) provide intimate ways to explore Panama's coastal landscapes. The calm waters of Gatun Lake, part of the Panama Canal system, offer a unique paddling experience. Glide past lush rainforest shores, keeping an eye out for howler monkeys, sloths, and exotic birds. In the San Blas Islands, kayak between pristine beaches and traditional Guna Yala communities, immersing yourself in both natural beauty and indigenous culture.

Fishing enthusiasts will find Panama a true angler's paradise. The waters off Piñas Bay in the Darien Gap are renowned for their abundance of black marlin and other big-game fish. Charter boats operate from the exclusive Tropic Star Lodge, offering world-class fishing experiences. For a more accessible option, try your luck in the Gulf of Chiriquí, where yellowfin tuna, dorado, and roosterfish await.

Beach lovers seeking pure relaxation will find their slice of paradise in the Pearl Islands. This archipelago in the Gulf of Panama boasts some of the country's most pristine beaches. Contadora Island, the most developed of the group, offers powdery white sand beaches like Playa Larga and Playa Cacique. Here, the hardest decision you'll face is whether to take another dip in the crystal-clear waters or order another fresh coconut drink.

For those who prefer their beaches with a side of luxury, the Pacific coast's Buenaventura delivers. This upscale resort area features a stunning stretch of golden sand, dotted with palm trees and high-end amenities. Visitors can indulge in beachfront spa treatments, enjoy gourmet dining with ocean views, or tee off at the nearby golf course.

Nature lovers shouldn't miss the chance to witness Panama's most magical beach experiences – sea turtle nesting. Playa Bluff on Isla Colón in Bocas del Toro is a crucial nesting site for leatherback turtles. Between April and September, visitors can join guided night tours to observe these ancient creatures laying their eggs or watch tiny hatchlings make their first journey to the sea.

Panama's commitment to marine conservation is evident in its protected areas. The Las Perlas Marine Special Management Zone safeguards the Pearl Islands' ecosystems, while the Coiba National Park preserves an extensive coral reef system in the Pacific. Responsible travelers can contribute to these efforts by choosing eco-friendly tour operators and practicing sustainable tourism.

When planning a Panamanian beach adventure, it's important to consider that the country's two coasts offer distinct experiences. The Caribbean side generally boasts calmer waters and powdery sand beaches, perfect for swimming and snorkeling. The Pacific coast, with its darker sand and more powerful waves, is ideal for surfing and sportfishing.

Whether you're seeking heart-pounding water sports action, serene beach relaxation, or a bit of both, Panama's diverse coastlines have something for every traveler. From the moment your toes touch the sand or you plunge into the warm waters, you'll understand why Panama is rapidly becoming a top destination for beach and water sport enthusiasts. So grab your sunscreen, pack your sense of adventure, and get ready to create unforgettable memories along Panama's spectacular shores.

Chapter 5: Cultural Immersion

Indigenous Communities

Panama's rich cultural landscape is deeply rooted in its indigenous heritage, with seven recognized indigenous groups calling this diverse country home. Each community offers a unique window into ancient traditions, vibrant artistry, and profound connections to the land. Travelers seeking authentic cultural experiences will find themselves captivated by the warmth, wisdom, and resilience of Panama's indigenous peoples.

The Guna (also known as Kuna) are perhaps the most well-known of Panama's indigenous groups, inhabiting the picturesque San Blas Islands and parts of the mainland in the Guna Yala comarca. Their colorful molas – intricately layered and hand-stitched textiles – have gained international recognition as symbols of Guna artistry and cultural identity. Visitors to Guna Yala can witness daily life in traditional villages, where thatched-roof huts line pristine beaches and dugout canoes ply the crystalline waters.

Guna communities maintain a high degree of autonomy, carefully managing tourism to preserve their way of life. When visiting, respect local customs by asking permission before taking photographs and dressing modestly. Many Guna islands offer basic accommodations, allowing travelers to immerse themselves in the rhythms of island life. Participate in traditional dance performances, learn about medicinal plant use, or simply engage in conversation with community members to gain deeper insights into Guna culture.

In western Panama, the Ngäbe and Buglé peoples inhabit the mountainous regions of Chiriquí, Veraguas, and Bocas del Toro. These communities are renowned for their distinctive chaquira beadwork and hand-woven nagua dresses. The annual Feria de la Naranja in Changuinola showcases Ngäbe-Buglé culture through traditional music, dance, and artisanal crafts. Visitors can support local economies by purchasing authentic handicrafts directly from artisans.

For an immersive experience in Ngäbe territory, consider a visit to the Soloy area near Boquete. Here, community-based tourism initiatives offer guided hikes through cloud forests, demonstrations of traditional farming techniques, and opportunities to participate in cacao harvesting and chocolate-making workshops. These experiences not only provide economic benefits to indigenous communities but also foster cross-cultural understanding and appreciation.

The Emberá and Wounaan peoples traditionally inhabit the dense rainforests of the Darién region and along the banks of the Chagres River. Known for their intricate basket weaving and body painting using natural pigments, these communities offer day trips from Panama City that provide a glimpse into their traditional lifestyles. Visitors can journey up the Chagres River in dugout canoes, welcomed by the haunting melodies of traditional flutes and drums.

In Emberá villages, guests may participate in body painting ceremonies, learn about medicinal plants used for centuries, and witness masterful demonstrations of basket weaving using local fibers. Sharing a traditional meal of fresh fish wrapped in banana leaves while seated on the floor of a communal hut creates lasting connections and memories. When visiting, bring small denominations of cash to purchase handicrafts directly from artisans, supporting local economies and preserving traditional skills.

The Naso people, also known as the Teribe, live along the Teribe River in Bocas del Toro province. The Naso, among Panama's smallest indigenous groups, are working to preserve their language and traditions while adapting to modern challenges. Visitors can arrange multi-day stays in Naso communities, participating in river fishing, learning about traditional plant medicines, and hiking through the lush forests of La Amistad International Park.

The Naso are actively involved in conservation efforts, recognizing the vital link between their cultural survival and the preservation of their ancestral lands. By engaging with Naso communities, travelers gain insights into sustainable living practices and the importance of maintaining biodiversity. Consider joining a Naso-led reforestation project or participating in traditional agricultural activities to deepen your understanding of their connection to the land.

In the eastern reaches of Panama, the Guna Madungandí and Guna Wargandí communities maintain their distinct identities while sharing cultural similarities with their San Blas cousins. These inland Guna groups face unique challenges as they balance tradition with encroaching development. Visits to these communities are less common but can be arranged through specialized tour operators committed to responsible tourism practices.

When exploring indigenous territories, it's crucial to approach these experiences with humility, respect, and a genuine desire to learn. Remember that you're entering people's homes and communities, not theme parks or living museums. Dress modestly, ask permission before taking photographs, and be mindful of local customs and taboos. Many communities have specific guidelines for visitors – adhere to these to ensure a positive experience for both guests and hosts.

Language barriers may exist, so consider hiring a reputable guide who can facilitate meaningful interactions and provide cultural context. Many indigenous communities have established their own tourism cooperatives or work with trusted tour operators. Opting for these community-led initiatives ensures that tourism benefits flow directly to the people you're visiting.

Participating in traditional ceremonies or rituals can be a profound experience, but always follow the guidance of community leaders. Some practices may be sacred or restricted to community members only. Express gratitude for the experiences shared with you, and be open to having your perspectives challenged and expanded.

Supporting indigenous communities extends beyond your visit. Purchase handicrafts directly from artisans when possible, ensuring fair compensation for their skills and materials. Learn about the challenges facing indigenous peoples in Panama – from land rights issues to cultural preservation efforts – and consider supporting reputable organizations working in partnership with these communities.

Embarking on a journey into Panama's indigenous heartlands requires cultivating an open mind and an open heart. These encounters have the power to transform not just your understanding of Panama, but your worldview as a whole. The wisdom, resilience, and deep connection to nature embodied by Panama's indigenous peoples offer valuable lessons for all of us navigating an increasingly complex world.

By approaching these cultural exchanges with respect, curiosity, and a willingness to listen, you'll forge meaningful connections that transcend linguistic and cultural barriers. The memories of sharing laughter with Guna children, the taste of freshly prepared Emberá cuisine, or the quiet wisdom imparted by a Naso elder will linger long after your return home. These experiences remind us of our shared humanity and the rich tapestry of human culture that makes our world so beautifully diverse.

Embarking on a journey through Panama's indigenous territories promises to move, challenge, and inspire travelers. The insights gained and connections forged will enrich your travels immeasurably, offering a depth of experience that goes far beyond typical tourist encounters. Embrace this opportunity for genuine cultural exchange, and allow the warmth and wisdom of Panama's indigenous peoples to touch your heart and broaden your horizons.

Festivals and Events

Panama's vibrant culture comes alive through its diverse festivals and events, offering travelers a chance to immerse themselves in the country's rich traditions, pulsating rhythms, and joyous celebrations. From colorful indigenous gatherings to lively street parades and solemn religious observances, the Panamanian calendar brims with opportunities to experience the heart and soul of this captivating nation.

January kicks off the year with a bang as the small town of Boquete in Chiriquí province hosts its annual Feria de las Flores y del Café (Flower and Coffee Fair). This 10-day extravaganza showcases the region's renowned coffee production and stunning floral displays. Visitors can sample artisanal brews, marvel at intricate flower arrangements, and enjoy live music performances against the backdrop of Boquete's misty mountains. The fair's vibrant atmosphere and enticing aromas create an unforgettable sensory experience.

February brings the electrifying energy of Carnival, Panama's most anticipated celebration. While Rio de Janeiro and New Orleans may be more famous for their Carnival festivities, Panama's version holds its own with four days of non-stop music, dancing, and elaborate parades. The action centers in Las Tablas, a small town in the Los Santos province, where two rival streets compete for the title of best float and most beautiful Carnival Queen. Revelers are doused with water from giant "culecos" (tanker trucks), providing welcome relief from the scorching summer heat. Panama City and other towns across the country also host their own Carnival celebrations, each with a unique local flavor.

As March arrives, the focus shifts to the Feria Internacional de David in Chiriquí province. This agricultural fair ranks among the largest in Central America, drawing visitors and exhibitors from across the region. Traditional livestock shows and agricultural displays sit alongside modern technology exhibits, creating a fascinating blend of rural tradition and contemporary innovation. The fair's festive atmosphere is enhanced by folk dance performances, live music, and an abundance of local culinary delights.

April brings the solemnity and tradition of Semana Santa (Holy Week), with religious processions and ceremonies taking place throughout the country. The colonial town of Villa de Los Santos in the Azuero Peninsula is particularly renowned for its Good Friday procession, where penitents dressed in purple robes carry heavy statues through the streets. The mixture of Catholic and indigenous traditions creates a uniquely Panamanian expression of faith and cultural identity.

May heralds the arrival of the Festival de Cristo Negro in Portobelo, Colón province. This celebration honors the Black Christ of Portobelo, a wooden statue that has been venerated for centuries. Pilgrims from across Panama and beyond flock to the small coastal town, many crawling on their knees to the statue's shrine in acts of devotion or gratitude. The festival's blend of religious fervor and cultural significance offers a powerful glimpse into Panama's spiritual heart.

June brings a burst of patriotic pride with Día de la Bandera (Flag Day) on June 4th. While not a public holiday, the day is marked by flag-raising ceremonies and patriotic displays across the country. Schools and public institutions often organize special events to commemorate the adoption of the Panamanian flag in 1925.

As July unfolds, the Feria del Manito in Ocú, Herrera province, celebrates the region's agricultural heritage and cowboy culture. This week-long fair showcases traditional cattle ranching techniques, folk music, and dance performances. Visitors can marvel at skilled horsemen demonstrating their prowess, sample local delicacies, and perhaps even try their hand at lassoing.

August is a month of national pride, with Independence from Spain Day on August 15th kicking off nearly three months of patriotic celebrations. Parades, fireworks, and cultural events mark this important historical milestone. The month also sees the vibrant Festival Nacional de la Mejorana in Guararé, Los Santos province. This four-day event is a feast for the senses, featuring traditional music, dance, and crafts from across Panama. The festival's highlight is the crowning of the Festival Queen, who must demonstrate proficiency in folk dances and play the mejorana, a small five-stringed guitar.

September continues the patriotic theme with Día de los Mártires (Martyrs' Day) on the 9th, commemorating a 1964 student uprising that played a crucial role in Panama's path to full sovereignty over the Canal Zone. The month culminates with the Feria de la Chorrera in Panama Oeste province, a agricultural and cultural fair that showcases the region's diverse products and traditions.

October brings a whirlwind of celebrations, starting with the Feria del Mar (Sea Fair) in Bocas del Toro. This event highlights the province's rich marine biodiversity and Afro-Caribbean culture through music, dance, and culinary exhibitions. Mid-month sees the Festival Nacional del Sombrero Pintao in La Pintada, Coclé province, celebrating the intricate art of hat-making that has been practiced in the region for generations. The month concludes with nationwide celebrations for Separation Day on October 28th, marking Panama's independence from Colombia in 1903.

November is punctuated by a series of independence-related holidays, with Flag Day on the 4th, the Primer Grito de Independencia de la Villa de Los Santos on the 10th, and Independence Day from Spain on the 28th. Each of these dates is marked by parades, cultural performances, and patriotic displays across the country. The picturesque mountain town of El Valle de Antón also hosts its annual orchid festival this month, showcasing the incredible diversity of these delicate flowers.

The year draws to a close with December's Feria de Artesanía in Panama City, a massive craft fair that brings together artisans from across the country. This event offers a perfect opportunity to purchase unique, handmade souvenirs while supporting local craftspeople. The holiday season culminates in joyous Christmas and New Year's Eve celebrations, with families gathering for traditional meals and festive parties lighting up the night sky.

Throughout the year, Panama's indigenous communities host their own celebrations, many of which are open to respectful visitors. The Guna people of the San Blas Islands celebrate the Nogagope festival in February, marking young women's coming of age with elaborate ceremonies and feasts. In December, the Emberá and Wounaan peoples of the Darién region hold their annual cultural congress, featuring traditional dances, music, and handicraft displays.

Experiencing Panama's festivals and events offers travelers a unique opportunity to connect with the country's vibrant culture and warm-hearted people. From the pulsating rhythms of Carnival to the solemn processions of Semana Santa, each celebration provides a window into the diverse traditions that shape Panama's national identity. By participating in these events, visitors not only create lasting memories but also contribute to the preservation and appreciation of Panama's rich cultural heritage.

When planning a Panamanian adventure, consider timing the visit to coincide with one or more of these remarkable celebrations. Whether you find yourself caught up in the frenetic energy of Carnival, moved by the devotion displayed during religious festivals, or marveling at the skill of traditional artisans, Panama's events calendar promises experiences that will touch your heart and ignite your senses. Embrace the festive spirit, engage with locals, and allow yourself to be swept away by the passion and pride that infuse these cherished traditions.

Panamanian Cuisine

Panamanian cuisine is a tantalizing fusion of flavors, reflecting the country's diverse cultural heritage and bountiful natural resources. From sizzling street food to sophisticated restaurant fare, Panama's culinary landscape offers a mouthwatering journey through history, tradition, and innovation. Prepare your taste buds for an unforgettable gastronomic adventure as we explore the rich tapestry of Panamanian dishes, ingredients, and dining experiences.

At the heart of Panamanian cuisine lies the humble yet versatile corn. This staple ingredient takes center stage in many traditional dishes, perhaps most famously in the form of tortillas. Unlike their Mexican counterparts, Panamanian tortillas are thick, hearty discs of corn dough, often served as a satisfying breakfast alongside eggs, cheese, and meat. The aroma of freshly cooked tortillas wafting through local markets is an irresistible invitation to start your day the Panamanian way.

Another corn-based delight is the tamale, known locally as tamal. These parcels of corn dough stuffed with meat, vegetables, and spices, then wrapped in banana leaves and steamed, are a beloved treat often enjoyed during holidays and special occasions. The process of unwrapping a tamal is like opening a fragrant gift, releasing a cloud of steam and revealing the savory treasure within.

Rice, beans, and plantains form the holy trinity of Panamanian cuisine, appearing in countless dishes across the country. Gallo pinto, a flavorful mix of rice and beans, often accompanies main dishes, while patacones – crispy fried plantain slices – serve as a popular side or snack. The comforting combination of these staples creates a satisfying base for many meals, with variations found from bustling city eateries to rural home kitchens.

Seafood plays a starring role in Panamanian cuisine, thanks to the country's expansive coastlines. Ceviche, a refreshing dish of raw fish or seafood "cooked" in citrus juices and spiced with onions and peppers, is a must-try. While many Latin American countries claim ceviche as their own, Panama's version often features corvina (sea bass) and is served with a side of patacones or salty crackers. Head to Panama City's Mercado de Mariscos to sample some of the freshest ceviche in the country, washed down with a cold beer or coconut water sipped straight from the fruit.

For a heartier seafood experience, seek out sancocho de mariscos, a rich seafood stew brimming with an assortment of fish, shellfish, and root vegetables in a flavorful broth. This dish perfectly encapsulates Panama's coastal bounty and is best enjoyed with a view of the ocean, perhaps at a rustic seafood shack among the many dotting the Pacific coast.

Meat lovers will find plenty to savor in Panamanian cuisine. Ropa vieja, which translates to "old clothes," is a comforting dish of shredded beef slow-cooked with tomatoes, peppers, and spices. Despite its humble appearance, the depth of flavor in this dish is truly remarkable. Another meaty favorite is tasajo, salt-cured beef that's rehydrated and cooked until tender, often served with rice and beans.

No exploration of Panamanian cuisine would be complete without mentioning sancocho, the national dish. This hearty chicken soup, packed with root vegetables, corn, and herbs, is more than just a meal – it's a cultural institution. Believed to have restorative powers, sancocho is often prepared for large family gatherings or to nurse someone back to health. The aroma of sancocho simmering on the stove evokes feelings of home and comfort for many Panamanians.

Street food in Panama offers a delicious way to sample local flavors on the go. Empanadas, crispy half-moon pastries filled with meat, cheese, or vegetables, make for a perfect quick snack. Carimañolas, yuca fritters stuffed with seasoned ground meat, offer a satisfying blend of crispy exterior and savory filling. For something sweet, try raspados, shaved ice topped with fruity syrups and condensed milk – a refreshing treat on a hot Panamanian day.

Panama's tropical climate yields an abundance of exotic fruits, many of which find their way into traditional desserts and drinks. Tres leches cake, a sponge cake soaked in three types of milk and often topped with fresh fruit, is a popular sweet treat. Chicheme, a creamy corn-based drink flavored with cinnamon and vanilla, offers a unique taste of Panama's indigenous heritage.

To truly immerse yourself in Panamanian cuisine, venture beyond the tourist hotspots and seek out local fondas – small, family-run eateries serving home-style meals. These unpretentious establishments often offer the most authentic and flavorful dishes at wallet-friendly prices. In Panama City, the Calidonia neighborhood is home to numerous fondas where you can sample daily specials scrawled on chalkboards and rub elbows with local office workers on their lunch breaks.

For a more upscale dining experience that still honors traditional flavors, Panama City boasts a growing number of innovative restaurants. Chefs are putting modern spins on classic dishes, using locally sourced ingredients to create exciting fusion cuisines. Restaurants like Maito and Intimo have garnered international acclaim for their creative interpretations of Panamanian culinary heritage.

Venturing outside the capital, each region of Panama offers its own culinary specialties. In the Chiriquí highlands, the cool climate allows for the cultivation of strawberries, giving rise to delightful desserts and preserves. The Caribbean coast, with its Afro-Antillean influences, serves up spicy stews and coconut-infused dishes that contrast with the milder flavors found elsewhere in the country.

To truly appreciate Panamanian cuisine, consider taking a cooking class or food tour. Many operators now offer hands-on experiences where you can learn to make traditional dishes, visit local markets to select ingredients, and gain insights into the cultural significance of various foods. These experiences not only provide valuable skills but also create lasting memories and a deeper connection to Panama's culinary traditions.

Panamanian cuisine is a reflection of the country's diverse history and abundant natural resources. An account of cultural interchange, adaptation, and invention is told by every meal. From the humble corn tortilla to elaborate seafood feasts, the flavors of Panama offer a delicious way to connect with the country's heart and soul.

Exploring Panama's culinary landscape requires an open mind and adventurous spirit for each meal. Allow the aromas, textures, and flavors to transport you, creating sensory memories that will linger long after your journey ends. Whether you're savoring a homecooked meal in a rural village or indulging in fine dining in Panama City, remember that each bite is a celebration of Panama's rich cultural heritage and the warmth of its people.

So pull up a chair, grab a fork (or your fingers, as many dishes are best enjoyed!), and prepare to embark on a gastronomic adventure through Panama. From the first sip of morning coffee to the last bite of a sweet dessert, let the flavors of this vibrant country enchant your palate and nourish your soul. Buen provecho!

Arts and Crafts

Panama's rich cultural heritage comes alive through its vibrant arts and crafts scene. From intricate textiles to masterful woodwork, the country's artisans continue to preserve and innovate traditional techniques passed down through generations. Exploring Panama's artistic landscape offers visitors a unique opportunity to connect with the country's diverse cultures and bring home truly meaningful souvenirs.

The iconic Panama hat, ironically of Ecuadorian origin, has become synonymous with the country. However, Panama boasts its own unique hat-making tradition in the form of the sombrero pintao. These meticulously crafted straw hats, woven from natural fibers, are adorned with intricate black and white geometric patterns. The small town of La Pintada in Coclé province is the epicenter of this craft, where skilled artisans spend weeks creating a single hat. Watching the nimble fingers of a master weaver at work is a mesmerizing experience, revealing the patience and precision required for this art form.

To truly appreciate the sombrero pintao, visit during the annual Festival Nacional del Sombrero Pintao held in La Pintada each October. This lively event showcases the finest examples of the craft, with competitions, demonstrations, and the opportunity to purchase directly from artisans. The festival's festive atmosphere, complete with traditional music and dance performances, offers a perfect backdrop to immerse yourself in this important aspect of Panamanian culture.

Perhaps the most internationally recognized Panamanian craft is the mola, a colorful textile art form created by the Guna people of the San Blas Islands. These intricate panels, traditionally used in women's blouses, feature layer upon layer of brightly colored fabric, cut and stitched to create stunning designs. Mola patterns often depict local flora and fauna, mythological figures, or scenes from daily life. The complexity and vibrancy of molas make them highly sought-after souvenirs and art pieces.

To witness mola-making firsthand and purchase authentic pieces, consider a visit to the Guna Yala comarca. Many Guna communities welcome respectful visitors, offering the chance to watch artisans at work and learn about the cultural significance of mola designs. In Panama City, the YMCA Handicraft Market and the Museo de la Mola provide excellent opportunities to browse and purchase high-quality molas while learning about their history and symbolism.

The Emberá and Wounaan peoples of Panama's Darién region are renowned for their exquisite basket weaving and wood carving. Using natural fibers from the chunga and nahuala palms, these artisans create baskets, plates, and decorative objects of astounding intricacy. The fine, tight weave of these pieces allows them to hold water, showcasing the remarkable skill involved in their creation. Emberá and Wounaan woodcarvings, often depicting animals or spirits, are equally impressive, with smooth surfaces and intricate details that seem to bring the figures to life.

To experience these crafts up close, consider a day trip to an Emberá village along the Chagres River, easily accessible from Panama City. Here, you can watch artisans at work, participate in traditional body painting using natural pigments, and purchase authentic crafts directly from their creators. The Museo de Penonomé in Coclé province also houses an excellent collection of indigenous crafts, providing context for the various techniques and cultural significance of these art forms.

In the western province of Chiriquí, the Ngäbe people are known for their colorful chaquiras – intricate beadwork used in jewelry and decorative objects. These vibrant pieces often incorporate traditional geometric patterns and symbols, with each design holding specific cultural meanings. The annual Feria de la Naranja in Changuinola, Bocas del Toro province, is an excellent opportunity to see and purchase Ngäbe crafts while enjoying the festive atmosphere of this cultural celebration.

Panama's pottery tradition dates back thousands of years, with pre-Columbian ceramics providing insight into ancient cultures. Today, the town of La Arena in Herrera province is known as the pottery capital of Panama. Here, artisans continue to use traditional techniques to create both decorative and functional pieces. Visitors can tour workshops, try their hand at the potter's wheel, and purchase unique, handcrafted items. The earthy tones and simple yet elegant designs of La Arena pottery make for beautiful and practical souvenirs.

Textile arts flourish throughout Panama, with each region boasting its own distinctive styles. In the Azuero Peninsula, the pollera – Panama's national dress – represents the pinnacle of traditional needlework. These elaborate dresses, adorned with intricate embroidery and lace, can take months or even years to complete. While full polleras are a significant investment, visitors can purchase smaller items like embroidered blouses or decorative pieces that showcase this exquisite handiwork.

The art of tembleques – delicate hair ornaments worn with the pollera – is another notable Panamanian craft. These shimmering accessories, often crafted from fish scales, pearls, or sequins, require immense patience and skill to create. Workshops in Las Tablas and other towns in the Azuero Peninsula offer the chance to see tembleque makers at work and purchase these unique pieces of wearable art.

For a comprehensive overview of Panama's artistic heritage, the Museo de Arte Contemporáneo in Panama City is a must-visit destination. This museum showcases both traditional and contemporary Panamanian art, providing context for the country's evolving creative landscape. The museum's gift shop offers a curated selection of high-quality crafts and artwork, making it an excellent spot for last-minute souvenir shopping.

Panama City's Casco Viejo neighborhood has emerged as a hub for artisanal crafts and design. Boutiques and galleries lining the historic streets offer a mix of traditional and contemporary items, from handwoven textiles to modern interpretations of indigenous designs. The area's vibrant atmosphere and beautiful colonial architecture make for a pleasant shopping experience, with plenty of cafes and restaurants to break up your exploration.

For those seeking an immersive craft experience, numerous workshops and classes are available throughout Panama. Learn the basics of mola-making in Guna Yala, try your hand at pottery in La Arena, or join a basket-weaving class with Emberá artisans. These hands-on experiences not only provide a deeper appreciation for the skill involved in creating these crafts but also offer a unique way to connect with local cultures and traditions.

When purchasing crafts and artwork in Panama, it's important to be mindful of authenticity and ethical considerations. Look for items made by indigenous artisans or local cooperatives, which ensure that your purchase directly supports the communities preserving these traditional crafts. Be wary of mass-produced imitations, particularly of items like molas, which are sometimes machine-printed rather than hand-stitched.

Panama's arts and crafts scene is a vivid reflection of the country's cultural diversity and rich artistic heritage. From the precise geometry of a sombrero pintao to the bold colors of a Guna mola, each piece tells a story of tradition, innovation, and cultural pride. By engaging with local artisans, visiting workshops, and thoughtfully selecting handcrafted souvenirs, travelers can play a role in preserving and celebrating Panama's artistic traditions.

Exploring the world of Panamanian arts and crafts reveals captivating displays of skill, creativity, and cultural significance embodied in each piece. Whether you're watching a master weaver at work, running your fingers over the smooth surface of a wooden carving, or adorning yourself with a beautifully embroidered textile, these experiences offer a tangible connection to Panama's heart and soul. The crafts you bring home will serve as lasting reminders of your journey, each item holding within it the warmth, color, and rich cultural tapestry of this remarkable country.

Chapter 6: Itineraries: Exploring Panama

3-Day Panama City Stopover

A 3-day stopover in Panama City offers an exhilarating glimpse into the vibrant heart of this diverse country. From colonial charm to modern marvels, culinary delights to cultural treasures, this compact itinerary packs in the essence of Panama's capital. Get ready for an unforgettable adventure that will leave you yearning to return and explore more of this captivating destination.

Day 1: Casco Viejo and Modern Panama City

Morning: Begin your Panama City experience in the historic district of Casco Viejo. Wake up early to beat the heat and crowds, starting your day with a steaming cup of Panamanian coffee at a charming cafe lining the cobblestone streets. The aroma of freshly brewed beans mingling with the salty sea air sets the perfect tone for your exploration.

When wandering through Casco Viejo's narrow streets, you'll be transported back in time. The neighborhood's pastel-colored buildings, wrought-iron balconies, and flower-filled plazas create a romantic atmosphere that's a photographer's dream. Don't miss the Metropolitan Cathedral, an architectural gem that took over 108 years to complete. Its gleaming white facade and twin bell towers dominate the skyline of this UNESCO World Heritage site.

Continue your morning with a visit to the Panama Canal Museum, housed in a beautifully restored building that once served as the headquarters for the French and American canal efforts. The museum's exhibits offer fascinating insights into the monumental task of building the canal and its impact on Panama's history and identity.

Afternoon: After lunch at a trendy Casco Viejo restaurant (try Fonda Lo Que Hay for innovative takes on traditional Panamanian dishes), it's time to contrast the old with the new. Head to the Miraflores Visitor Center at the Panama Canal for an up-close look at this engineering marvel in action. Time your visit to coincide with a ship passing through the locks – the sight of massive vessels being raised and lowered is truly awe-inspiring.

Evening: As the sun sets, make your way to the Amador Causeway for breathtaking views of the city skyline and the Bridge of the Americas. This palm-lined stretch connecting four small islands offers a perfect spot for an evening stroll or bike ride. Enjoy dinner at a waterfront restaurant, savoring fresh seafood while watching ships queue up to enter the canal.

Day 2: Nature and Culture

Morning: Start your day with an early morning visit to the Metropolitan Natural Park, a vast tropical forest right in the heart of the city. While hiking the trails, keep an eye out for sloths, toucans, and howler monkeys – the park is home to an incredible diversity of wildlife. The view of the city skyline juxtaposed against the lush greenery from the park's Mirador offers a unique perspective on Panama City's blend of urban development and natural beauty.

After your nature walk, dive into Panama's cultural heritage at the Museo del Canal Interoceánico. This museum, located in a beautifully restored building in Casco Viejo, offers a comprehensive look at Panama's history, from pre-Columbian times through the construction of the canal and beyond. The exhibits bring to life the struggles and triumphs that have shaped the nation.

Afternoon: Dedicate your afternoon to exploring Panama's vibrant art scene. Start at the Museo de Arte Contemporáneo, which showcases both Panamanian and international modern art. The museum's collection offers insights into how contemporary artists are interpreting Panama's complex identity and rapid development.

Next, head to the Diablo Rosso gallery in Casco Viejo, a cutting-edge space that represents some of Panama's most exciting young artists. The gallery's innovative exhibitions and events make it a hub for the city's creative community.

Evening: As night falls, it's time to experience Panama City's culinary scene. Book a table at Maito, consistently ranked among Latin America's best restaurants. Chef Mario Castrellón's innovative menu celebrates Panama's biodiversity, incorporating ingredients from the country's various ecosystems into refined, creative dishes. The tasting menu is a culinary journey through Panama's landscapes and cultures.

After dinner, if you're up for it, check out the nightlife in the trendy Calle Uruguay area. From laid-back bars to high-energy clubs, there's something for every taste.

Day 3: Canal Zone and Shopping

Morning: On your final day, venture out to the Gamboa Rainforest Reserve, about an hour from the city center. Take an aerial tram ride through the forest canopy for a bird's-eye view of the lush ecosystem. Follow this with a boat tour on Gatun Lake, part of the Panama Canal. You'll likely spot capuchin monkeys, crocodiles, and a wide variety of tropical birds. The contrast between the tranquil natural setting and the massive cargo ships passing through the canal is striking.

Afternoon: Return to the city for some last-minute shopping and souvenir hunting. The Mercado de Artesanías in Balboa is a great place to find traditional crafts from across Panama. Look for colorful molas (textiles made by the Guna people), tagua nut carvings, and Panama hats (which, despite the name, originated in Ecuador).

For a more modern shopping experience, visit the Multiplaza Pacific mall. This upscale shopping center offers a mix of international brands and local boutiques. It's also a good place to cool off in the air conditioning if the tropical heat is getting to you.

Evening: Cap off your Panama City adventure with a sunset visit to the Biomuseo, designed by renowned architect Frank Gehry. The museum's colorful, unconventional design is a landmark in itself, and its exhibits tell the story of Panama's crucial role in the Earth's biodiversity. The view of the sun setting over the Pacific Ocean from the museum's gardens is a perfect way to reflect on your whirlwind tour of this dynamic city.

For your final dinner, head back to Casco Viejo and find a table at Donde José. This intimate restaurant offers an innovative tasting menu that takes diners on a journey through Panama's culinary heritage. It's a fitting end to your exploration of Panama City's many facets.

Logistics:

- **Accommodation:** Stay in or near Casco Viejo for easy access to many attractions and a charming atmosphere. Hotels like the American Trade Hotel or Central Hotel Panama offer luxury in historic buildings, while boutique options like La Concordia provide character and comfort.

- **Transportation:** Use a mix of walking (especially in Casco Viejo), taxis, and Uber for getting around. The Metro is useful for longer trips within the city.

- **Weather:** the entire year is hot and muggy in Panama City. Start your days early, carry water, and plan for afternoon breaks to avoid the peak heat.

- **Language:** While English is widely spoken in tourist areas, learning a few basic Spanish phrases will enhance your experience and interactions with locals.

This 3-day itinerary offers a taste of Panama City's diverse attractions, from its rich history and culture to its natural beauty and modern developments. The blend of colonial charm, tropical wilderness, and cosmopolitan energy creates a unique urban experience that will leave you with lasting memories and a desire to explore more of what Panama has to offer. Whether you're marveling at ships passing through the canal, sampling innovative Panamanian cuisine, or spotting wildlife just minutes from the city center, Panama City promises an adventure that engages all your senses and challenges your preconceptions of Central America.

7-Day Panama Highlights Tour

A 7-day Panama highlights tour offers an immersive journey through the country's diverse landscapes, rich culture, and vibrant communities. This carefully crafted itinerary takes you beyond the capital city, allowing you to experience the true essence of Panama. From lush rainforests to pristine beaches, colonial towns to indigenous communities, prepare for an adventure that will captivate your senses and leave you with unforgettable memories.

Day 1: Arrival in Panama City and Embera Village Visit

Morning: Upon arrival at Tocumen International Airport, you'll be greeted by the warm, humid air of Panama. After settling into your hotel, waste no time in diving into Panama's cultural diversity with a visit to an Embera indigenous village along the Chagres River.

A short drive and scenic boat ride will transport you into the heart of the rainforest. Upon nearing the village, the sound of traditional flutes and drums will greet visitors. The Embera people, known for their vibrant body paint and colorful attire, will introduce you to their way of life.

Participate in a traditional dance, learn about medicinal plants used for centuries, and try your hand at crafting intricate baskets.

Afternoon: Enjoy a lunch of fresh fish wrapped in banana leaves, prepared by the community. This is an opportunity to engage with community members, learning about their challenges and triumphs in preserving their culture in the modern world.

Before leaving, browse the handcrafted items for sale - the intricate beadwork and tagua nut carvings make for unique souvenirs that directly support the community.

Evening: Return to Panama City and enjoy a relaxing dinner at a local restaurant, perhaps trying the national dish, sancocho, a hearty chicken soup that's perfect for replenishing your energy after a day of cultural immersion.

Day 2: San Blas Islands Adventure

Early Morning: Rise before dawn for a flight to the San Blas Islands, an archipelago of over 365 islands in the Caribbean Sea. Governed by the Guna people, this autonomous region offers a glimpse into a unique way of life and some of the most beautiful beaches in the world.

Upon arrival, you'll be struck by the postcard-perfect scenery - crystal-clear turquoise waters lapping against white sand beaches fringed with palm trees. Spend the morning island-hopping, snorkeling among vibrant coral reefs teeming with tropical fish.

Afternoon: Visit a Guna community to learn about their matriarchal society and the art of mola-making. These intricate textiles, featuring layers of colorful fabric stitched into elaborate designs, are central to Guna culture. Watch skilled artisans at work and perhaps purchase a mola directly from its creator.

Evening: As the sun sets, enjoy a beachside dinner of freshly caught seafood. If you're lucky, you might witness the bioluminescent plankton that sometimes illuminate the waters at night, creating a magical, starry effect in the sea.

Day 3: Boquete and Coffee Plantations

Morning: Take an early flight to David, then drive to the charming mountain town of Boquete in Chiriquí province. Known for its eternal spring-like climate and lush scenery, Boquete is a stark contrast to the tropical lowlands.

Start your day with a visit to a local coffee plantation. Panama's Geisha coffee, grown in this region, is renowned as the finest and most expensive in the world. Tour the plantation, learning about the meticulous process of growing, harvesting, and roasting coffee beans.

The passion of the local farmers is palpable as they explain the nuances that make their coffee so special.

Afternoon: After lunch, embark on a hike in the cloud forests surrounding Boquete. The Sendero de los Quetzales trail offers breathtaking views and the chance to spot the resplendent quetzal, a strikingly beautiful bird sacred to ancient Mesoamerican cultures.

Evening: Savor dinner at a farm-to-table restaurant in Boquete, where chefs craft innovative dishes using locally sourced ingredients. The cool mountain air and serene atmosphere provide a perfect setting for reflecting on your day's adventures.

Day 4: Bocas del Toro Archipelago

Morning: Travel to the Caribbean archipelago of Bocas del Toro, a laid-back paradise known for its stunning beaches, diverse marine life, and Afro-Caribbean culture. Upon arrival, take a boat tour to Dolphin Bay, where you can observe playful bottlenose dolphins in their natural habitat.

Afternoon: Visit Isla Bastimentos National Marine Park, home to some of Panama's most beautiful beaches. Red Frog Beach, named for the tiny strawberry poison-dart frogs found there, offers a perfect spot for sunbathing and swimming. Snorkel around the coral reefs, marveling at the kaleidoscope of tropical fish darting among the corals.

Evening: Back in Bocas Town on Isla Colón, immerse yourself in the vibrant local culture. The town's colorful Caribbean-style buildings and lively street scenes create a festive atmosphere. Enjoy dinner at a waterfront restaurant, savoring fresh seafood and Afro-Caribbean flavors while listening to the rhythms of reggae and calypso music.

Day 5: Panama Canal Railway and Portobelo

Morning: Return to Panama City and embark on a scenic journey aboard the Panama Canal Railway. This historic train ride offers stunning views of the canal, lush rainforests, and Gatun Lake. The contrast between the engineering marvel of the canal and the untamed wilderness surrounding it is truly awe-inspiring.

Afternoon: Arrive in Colón and continue to the historic town of Portobelo. Once a crucial port for Spanish colonial trade, Portobelo's well-preserved fortifications are now a UNESCO World Heritage site. Explore the ruins of Fort San Lorenzo, imagining the battles between Spanish defenders and marauding pirates that once took place here.

Visit the Iglesia de San Felipe, home to the famous Black Christ statue. The church's simple exterior belies the profound spiritual significance it holds for many Panamanians.

Evening: Return to Panama City for a night of local cuisine and music. Visit the bustling Mercado de Mariscos for dinner, where you can sample an array of fresh seafood dishes. Try the local favorite, corvina al ajillo (sea bass in garlic sauce), or be adventurous with a ceviche mixto.

Day 6: El Valle de Antón

Morning: Drive to El Valle de Antón, a picturesque town nestled in the crater of an extinct volcano. The cool climate and lush surroundings make it a popular weekend retreat for city dwellers. Start your day with a visit to the local market, where you can find a variety of handicrafts, fresh produce, and medicinal plants.

Take a guided hike to the famous square trees, a mysterious natural phenomenon unique to this area. The trail also offers opportunities to spot exotic birds and butterflies.

Afternoon: Visit the El Nispero Zoo and Botanical Garden, home to the Golden Frog Conservation Center. These tiny, bright yellow frogs are Panama's national amphibian and are critically endangered. Learning about conservation efforts to save this species offers a poignant reminder of the fragility of Panama's ecosystems.

Relax in the thermal pools, letting the warm, mineral-rich waters soothe your muscles after days of exploration. The serene forest setting provides a perfect backdrop for reflection on your Panamanian journey.

Evening: Enjoy a farewell dinner at a local restaurant, savoring traditional Panamanian dishes while recounting the highlights of your trip with fellow travelers.

Day 7: Departure

Morning: Before departing, take one last stroll through a local neighborhood in Panama City. Visit a panadería (bakery) for some fresh-baked bread or pastries, chatting with locals as they go about their daily routines. This final glimpse of everyday Panamanian life will leave you with lasting impressions of the country's warmth and vibrancy.

Head to the airport, carrying with you a wealth of memories, new perspectives, and perhaps a few handcrafted souvenirs. The diverse experiences of the past week - from indigenous villages to Caribbean islands, cloud forests to colonial fortresses - will have given you a deep appreciation for Panama's natural beauty, rich history, and cultural diversity.

Logistics:

- **Accommodation:** Mix of comfortable hotels in cities and eco-lodges in rural areas. In San Blas and Bocas del Toro, consider staying in over-water bungalows for a unique experience.
- **Transportation:** Combination of domestic flights, boat rides, and private transfers. The Panama Canal Railway offers a unique travel experience.
- **Packing:** Bring lightweight, breathable clothing for lowland areas, and warmer layers for Boquete and El Valle. Remember to bring a reusable water bottle, sunscreen, and insect repellent.
- **Health:** Ensure your vaccinations are up to date. Drink bottled water in rural areas.
- **Language:** While English is widely spoken in tourist areas, learning some basic Spanish phrases will enrich your interactions with locals.

This 7-day itinerary offers a comprehensive introduction to Panama's diverse attractions, from its vibrant indigenous cultures to its stunning natural landscapes. Each day brings new discoveries, challenging preconceptions and inspiring a deeper understanding of this multifaceted country. Whether you're marveling at the engineering of the Panama Canal, lounging on pristine Caribbean beaches, or hiking through misty cloud forests, Panama promises an adventure that will stay with you long after you've returned home. The warmth of its people, the richness of its ecosystems, and the depth of its history create a tapestry of experiences that showcase the very best of Central America.

Chapter 7: Practical Information

Language Tips

Let's talk about language tips that'll make your Panamanian adventure smoother and more enjoyable.

Spanish is the official language of Panama, and while you might encounter some English speakers in tourist areas, knowing a bit of Spanish will enhance your experience tremendously. It'll help you connect with locals, order food with confidence, and even haggle at markets like a pro!

Let's start with some essential Spanish phrases you'll want to have in your linguistic toolkit:

- "Hola" - Hello
- "Gracias" - Thank you
- "Por favor" - Please
- "De nada" - You're welcome
- "¿Cómo estás?" - How are you?
- "Muy bien, gracias" - Very well, thank you
- "¿Dónde está...?" - Where is...?
- "No entiendo" - I don't understand
- "¿Habla inglés?" - Do you speak English?
- "La cuenta, por favor" - The bill, please
- "¿Cuánto cuesta?" - How much does it cost?

- "Necesito ayuda" - I need help
- "Disculpe" - Excuse me
- "Baño" - Bathroom
- "Agua" - Water
- "Cerveza" - Beer (because you might want to relax on the beach!)

Now, let's get into some regional linguistic quirks you might encounter in Panama. Panamanians have their own unique slang and expressions that'll make you feel like a local if you use them:

- "Chuleta" - This literally means "pork chop," but in Panama, it's an expression of surprise, similar to "Wow!"
- "Que xopa" - A casual greeting, like "What's up?"
- "Pela'o" or "pela'a" - Refers to a young person, boy or girl
- "Bien care'tube" - Someone who's shameless or has a lot of nerve
- "Chantin" - House or home
- "Quédate tranquilo" - Take it easy, relax

Panamanians often drop the 's' at the end of words, so "gracias" might sound more like "gracia." They also tend to speak quickly, so don't be afraid to ask people to slow down: "¿Puede hablar más despacio, por favor?" (Can you speak more slowly, please?)

In Panama City, you'll find more English speakers, especially in business and tourist areas. However, venture into rural areas or smaller towns, and Spanish becomes essential. The indigenous communities in Panama, like the Guna and Emberá, have their own languages, but they typically speak Spanish as well.

When you're ordering food, knowing some local dish names will be incredibly helpful. Try asking for "sancocho" (a hearty chicken soup), "patacones" (fried plantains), or "ceviche" (a citrusy seafood dish). And don't forget to say "¡Buen provecho!" before eating - it's the Panamanian equivalent of "Bon appétit!"

Panamanian Spanish has a musical quality to it, with a rhythmic cadence that reflects the country's vibrant culture. You'll notice that Panamanians often use diminutives, adding "-ito" or "-ita" to words to make them sound friendlier or cuter. For example, "un momento" (one moment) becomes "un momentito."

Learning a few phrases about Panama's famous canal will surely impress locals. Try dropping "Las esclusas de Miraflores" (Miraflores Locks) or "El Canal de Panamá es una maravilla de ingeniería" (The Panama Canal is an engineering marvel) into conversation.

When you're out exploring Panama's stunning beaches, you might hear "está full" to describe a crowded place. This Spanglish term is widely used and understood.

Panamanians are generally warm and welcoming people. They appreciate it when visitors make an effort to speak Spanish, even if it's not perfect. Don't be shy about practicing your Spanish skills - most locals will be patient and happy to help you learn.

If you're planning to visit during a festival or holiday, learn some related phrases. For Carnival, you might hear "¡A gozar!" which means "Let's enjoy!" During Christmas, "Feliz Navidad" is a must-know phrase.

For nature lovers exploring Panama's lush rainforests, knowing words like "mono" (monkey), "perezoso" (sloth), or "quetzal" (a beautiful bird species) can enrich your experience.

When you're shopping at local markets, numbers are crucial. Practice counting in Spanish and learn how to ask "¿Hay descuento?" (Is there a discount?) - you never know when it might come in handy!

Lastly, remember that language is more than just words - it's about connection. A smile, a respectful attitude, and an eagerness to learn will take you far in Panama. Even if your Spanish isn't perfect, your efforts to communicate will be appreciated.

So, pack your bags, bring your Spanish phrasebook (or a good translation app), and get ready for an unforgettable Panamanian adventure. With these language tips in your arsenal, you're all set to explore the vibrant culture, stunning landscapes, and warm hospitality of Panama. ¡Buen viaje! (Have a good trip!)

Money Matters

Welcome to the Money Matters section of our Panama Travel Guide 2024-2025! Let's dive into the nitty-gritty of handling your finances while exploring this beautiful Central American gem.

First things first: currency. Panama uses two official currencies - the Panamanian Balboa (PAB) and the United States Dollar (USD). Here's the kicker: the Balboa is pegged to the US Dollar at a 1:1 ratio, and you'll mostly see US Dollars in circulation. Coins are a mix of Panamanian and US currency, but they're interchangeable due to the fixed exchange rate. This dual-currency system makes life easier for travelers from the US, but it might take some getting used to for others.

When it comes to cash, you'll find ATMs readily available in cities and tourist areas. However, always carry some backup cash, especially when venturing into rural regions. Most ATMs dispense US Dollars, and you can usually withdraw up to $500 per transaction. Be aware that some machines might charge a fee, typically around $5, so it's worth checking with your bank about international withdrawal fees before you leave.

Credit cards are widely accepted in hotels, restaurants, and larger stores, particularly in Panama City and tourist hotspots. Visa and Mastercard are the most commonly accepted, with American Express less so. However, small local shops, markets, and rural areas often operate on a cash-only basis, so keep that in mind when planning your adventures.

Banking services in Panama are modern and efficient, especially in urban areas. Major banks like Banco General, Banistmo, and Banco Nacional de Panamá offer services to tourists. If you need to exchange currency, banks usually offer better rates than hotels or exchange bureaus. Remember to bring your passport for any banking transactions.

Now, let's talk about tipping - a subject that can cause anxiety for many travelers. In Panama, tipping isn't as ingrained in the culture as it is in some countries, but it's becoming more common in tourist areas. Here's a quick guide:

- **Restaurants:** A 10% service charge is often included in the bill. If it's not, or if the service was exceptional, an additional 5-10% is appreciated.
- **Taxis:** Tipping isn't expected, but rounding up the fare is a nice gesture.
- **Hotels:** $1-2 per bag for porters, and $2-3 per day for housekeeping is standard.
- **Tour guides:** For a full-day tour, $10-20 per person is a good rule of thumb.

These are just guidelines. If someone goes above and beyond to make your experience special, feel free to show your appreciation accordingly.

Now, let's get into some budget-saving tips because who doesn't love stretching their travel dollars?

1. Eat like a local: Panama's fondas (small, family-run eateries) offer delicious, filling meals at a fraction of the cost of tourist restaurants. Look for the "plato del día" (plate of the day) for the best deals.

2. Use public transportation: Panama City has a modern metro system and reliable bus network. The metro is not only cheap but also a great way to avoid the city's notorious traffic jams.

3. Visit during the green season: From May to November, you'll find lower prices on accommodations and fewer crowds. Just be ready for the odd downpour of rain.

4. Stay in hostels or guesthouses: Panama has a range of budget-friendly accommodations that offer a chance to meet fellow travelers and get local tips.

5. Take advantage of free attractions: Many of Panama's best experiences don't cost a dime. Stroll through the historic Casco Viejo district, hike in metropolitan parks, or enjoy the vibrant street art scene.

6. Buy groceries: If you're staying somewhere with kitchen access, cooking some of your meals can significantly cut costs. Local markets are a feast for the senses and easy on the wallet.

7. Use local sim cards: Instead of paying for expensive international roaming, pick up a local sim card for cheap data and calls.

8. Negotiate at markets: When shopping for souvenirs, don't be afraid to haggle politely. It's often expected and can lead to better prices.

9. Take advantage of happy hours: Many bars and restaurants offer great deals during happy hour, usually in the early evening.

10. Book tours locally: While it's tempting to book everything in advance, you can often find better deals by booking tours and activities once you're in Panama.

One important note: while Panama is generally safe, exercise caution with your valuables, especially in crowded areas. Use hotel safes when available, and be discreet when using ATMs or handling cash in public.

For those planning extended stays or considering property investment, Panama offers attractive options like the Pensionado Visa program, which provides benefits to retirees. However, always consult with a local lawyer or financial advisor before making any significant financial commitments.

Lastly, keep an eye out for seasonal events that might affect prices. Carnival in February and November's independence celebrations can lead to higher costs in popular areas, but they also offer unforgettable experiences that might be worth the splurge.

Remember, managing your money wisely doesn't mean missing out on experiences. It's about making informed choices that allow you to enjoy all that Panama has to offer without breaking the bank. With these tips in your pocket, you're all set for an amazing Panamanian adventure that's rich in experiences and light on financial stress.

Communication and Internet

In today's hyper-connected world, staying in touch with loved ones and accessing information on the go is crucial for any traveler. Let's explore how you can keep your digital life humming while enjoying the stunning beaches, lush rainforests, and vibrant culture of Panama.

First, let's talk about phone services. Panama boasts a robust mobile network that covers most of the country, including popular tourist destinations. The main mobile operators are Más Móvil (formerly Cable & Wireless), Tigo (formerly Movistar), Digicel, and Claro. 4G LTE is widely available in urban areas and tourist hotspots, with 5G networks expanding rapidly, especially in Panama City.

If you're planning to use your phone from home, check with your provider about international roaming plans. While convenient, these can be expensive. A more budget-friendly option is to purchase a local SIM card upon arrival. You can easily find these at the Tocumen International Airport, shopping malls, or authorized dealer shops throughout the country.

Your passport is required in order to purchase a SIM card. Prepaid plans are the most flexible option for travelers, allowing you to top up credit as needed. Prices are reasonable, with packages offering ample data, local calls, and even some international minutes. For example, a typical tourist package might include 5GB of data, unlimited local calls, and 100 international minutes for about $15-20, valid for 15-30 days.

Now, let's dive into Wi-Fi availability. You'll be pleasantly surprised by how easy it is to find Wi-Fi in Panama, especially in urban areas and tourist destinations. Most hotels, hostels, cafes, and restaurants offer free Wi-Fi to customers. In Panama City, you'll even find free public Wi-Fi in many parks and public spaces - perfect for uploading those envy-inducing beach photos!

However, be cautious when using public Wi-Fi networks. They're convenient but not always secure. Consider using a VPN (Virtual Private Network) to protect your personal information when connecting to public networks. There are many reliable VPN apps available for both iOS and Android devices.

Speaking of apps, let's explore some that can make your Panamanian adventure smoother and more enjoyable:

1. WhatsApp: This messaging app is widely used in Panama for both personal and business communication. It's great for staying in touch with new local friends or contacting tour operators.

2. Google Maps: An essential for navigating Panama's cities and finding points of interest. Don't forget to download offline maps for areas with spotty coverage.

3. Uber: Available in Panama City and some other urban areas, Uber can be a convenient and safe way to get around.

4. PedidosYa or Appetito24: These food delivery apps are popular in Panama City and other major towns, perfect for those lazy evenings in your hotel.

5. XE Currency: With Panama using both the US Dollar and the Balboa, this currency converter can be handy, especially if you're visiting from outside the US.

6. Google Translate: While many Panamanians in tourist areas speak some English, this app can be a lifesaver in more remote regions.

7. iNaturalist: Great for nature lovers exploring Panama's incredible biodiversity. It assists in identifying flora and fauna that you come across.

8. AccuWeather or Weather Underground: Panama's weather can be unpredictable, especially during the rainy season. These apps provide accurate local forecasts.

9. Maps.me: An excellent offline map app, particularly useful for hiking or exploring off the beaten path.

Remember to download and set up these apps before you leave home. This way, you're ready to go as soon as you land in Panama.

Now, let's talk about some communication quirks and tips specific to Panama. Panamanians are generally warm and expressive communicators. Don't be surprised if your newfound local friends want to add you on social media or WhatsApp. It's a common way to keep in touch, even with people you've just met.

If you're working remotely during your stay, you'll find that Panama, especially Panama City, is becoming increasingly digital nomad-friendly. Many cafes and co-working spaces offer high-speed internet suitable for video calls and large file transfers. However, if you're heading to more remote areas or smaller islands, be prepared for potentially slower or less reliable connections.

One unique aspect of communication in Panama is the mix of Spanish and English, especially in business settings. You might hear Spanglish phrases thrown into conversation, reflecting the country's international influence, particularly due to the Panama Canal.

For emergency situations, it's crucial to know the local emergency numbers. In Panama, you can dial 911 for police, fire, or medical emergencies. Save this number in your phone, just in case.

Lastly, while digital communication is incredibly convenient, don't forget to unplug and fully immerse yourself in the Panamanian experience. Strike up conversations with locals at a neighborhood café, practice your Spanish with market vendors, or simply sit on a beach and soak in the stunning surroundings without the distraction of a screen.

Panama's combination of modern infrastructure and natural beauty creates a perfect backdrop for both staying connected and disconnecting at will. Whether you're sharing stunning photos of the Panama Canal, video calling family from a rainforest lodge, or simply enjoying the moment without digital distractions, you'll find that Panama offers the flexibility to communicate on your terms.

Charge up your devices, update your apps, and get ready for an unforgettable Panamanian adventure. With these communication tools at your fingertips, you're all set to create, share, and cherish memories that will last a lifetime. ¡Buen viaje y buena comunicación!

Packing Essentials

Ready to pack for your Panamanian adventure? Let's dive into the essentials you'll need to make your trip comfortable, enjoyable, and memorable. Panama's diverse landscapes and climate zones mean you'll need to pack smart to be prepared for everything from bustling city life to tropical beaches and misty cloud forests.

First, let's talk about clothing. Panama's climate is tropical, which means it's generally hot and humid year-round. Light, breathable fabrics are your best friends here. Bring an abundance of shorts, t-shirts, and airy dresses or skirts. Don't forget swimwear - you'll want to take advantage of Panama's beautiful beaches and pools!

Here's a basic clothing list to get you started:
- 5-7 t-shirts or tank tops
- 3-4 pairs of shorts
- 2-3 lightweight dresses or skirts
- 1-2 pairs of light pants or jeans (for cooler evenings or more conservative areas)
- 1 light jacket or sweater (for air-conditioned spaces or higher altitudes)
- 7+ pairs of underwear and socks
- 2-3 swimsuits
- 1 pair of pajamas
- 1 outfit for nicer occasions (restaurants, nightlife)

Footwear is crucial in Panama. You'll be doing a lot of walking, whether exploring Panama City's vibrant streets or hiking through lush rainforests. Pack:
- One pair of comfy sneakers or walking shoes
- 1 pair of sandals or flip-flops
- 1 pair of water shoes (great for rocky beaches or boat trips)
- Optional: 1 pair of dressier shoes for nights out

Now, let's talk about sun protection. Panama's proximity to the equator means the sun is intense. Don't skimp on:
- Sunscreen (SPF 30 or higher)
- Sunglasses
- Wide-brimmed hat or cap
- Lip balm with SPF

Insect repellent is another must-have, especially if you're planning to explore Panama's lush forests or spend time outdoors during dawn or dusk. Look for repellents containing DEET or picaridin for best results.

When it comes to toiletries, pack your usual essentials, but consider travel-sized options to save space. Don't forget:
- Shampoo and conditioner
- Body wash
- Toothbrush and toothpaste
- Deodorant

- Any personal medications
- Hand sanitizer
- Wet wipes (great for quick refreshes in the humid climate)

For tech and gadgets, consider bringing:

- Smartphone (don't forget the charger!)
- Camera (if you prefer higher quality photos than your phone can provide)
- Power bank
- Universal travel adapter (Panama uses the same outlets as the US, but it's handy if you're coming from elsewhere)
- Waterproof phone case (great for beach days or boat trips)

Now, let's get into some activity-specific items. If you're planning to hike or explore Panama's national parks, you'll want to pack:

- Lightweight, quick-dry hiking pants
- Moisture-wicking shirts
- Sturdy hiking boots or trail shoes
- Daypack
- Reusable water bottle
- Binoculars (for wildlife spotting)

For beach lovers, consider adding:

- Beach towel (or a quick-dry travel towel)

- Snorkel gear (you can rent this, but bringing your own ensures a good fit)
- Dry bag (to keep your belongings safe on boat trips or beach days)
- Beach cover-up

Don't forget about rainy season essentials if you're visiting between May and November:
- Lightweight rain jacket or poncho
- Quick-dry clothing
- Waterproof bag cover

A few more miscellaneous items that can come in handy: Small first aid kit (include any personal medications, pain relievers, band-aids, and anti-diarrhea medication)
- Reusable shopping bag (great for market trips and reducing plastic waste)
- Travel locks (for securing your luggage)
- Ziplock bags (useful for organizing and protecting items from humidity)
- Spanish phrasebook or language app

Panama City has plenty of shopping options if you forget anything, but prices for certain items (like sunscreen or insect repellent) can be higher than what you're used to at home.

When packing, consider using packing cubes or compression bags to maximize space in your luggage. Rolling your clothes instead of folding them can also help save space and reduce wrinkles.

If you're planning to visit multiple climate zones in Panama, layering is key. A lightweight, long-sleeved shirt can protect you from both sun and insects, and can be paired with a light jacket for cooler evenings in the highlands.

Don't overpack! Many hotels and hostels in Panama offer laundry services, and you can always wash a few items in your sink if needed. Leaving some space in your luggage also allows room for souvenirs - you might want to bring home some of Panama's famous molas (colorful textiles), coffee, or rum.

Don't forget the most important items: your passport, travel insurance documents, and any necessary visas or permits. It's a good idea to make copies of these and keep them separate from the originals.

Packing for Panama is all about balance - being prepared for various activities and climates while not weighing yourself down with unnecessary items. With this packing list, you'll be ready to explore Panama's stunning beaches, trek through its lush rainforests, and immerse yourself in its vibrant culture.

Take note, the joy of travel often comes from the unexpected experiences and connections you make along the way. While it's important to be prepared, don't stress too much about packing every single item. Panama is a welcoming country, and you'll be able to find most things you need if you forget something.

So zip up that suitcase, double-check your essentials, and get ready for an incredible Panamanian adventure. The diverse landscapes, rich culture, and warm people of Panama are waiting to welcome you.

Responsible Travel Tips

Let's explore how we can make our Panamanian adventures not just memorable, but also sustainable and respectful to the local environment, culture, and communities.

Panama is a country of breathtaking biodiversity, rich cultural heritage, and warm, welcoming people. By traveling responsibly, we can help preserve these treasures for future generations while deepening our own travel experiences. It's about creating positive impacts and meaningful connections, rather than just passing through as observers.

First, let's talk about environmental responsibility. Panama's ecosystems are incredibly diverse, from lush rainforests to pristine beaches and vibrant coral reefs. Here's how you can minimize your ecological footprint:

1. Say no to single-use plastics. Bring a reusable water bottle and shopping bag. Panama's tap water is generally safe to drink in urban areas, so you can easily refill your bottle.

2. Choose reef-safe sunscreen. Traditional sunscreens can harm coral reefs. Opt for mineral-based options that don't contain oxybenzone or octinoxate.

3. Stick to marked trails when hiking. This helps prevent erosion and protects sensitive plant life.

4. Practice responsible wildlife viewing. Keep a respectful distance from animals and never feed them. Use binoculars for a closer look instead of disturbing their natural behavior.

5. Support eco-friendly accommodations. Look for hotels and lodges that practice water and energy conservation, use renewable energy, and manage waste responsibly.

6. Participate in beach clean-ups. Many coastal communities organize these events, offering a chance to give back while connecting with locals.

Now, let's dive into cultural responsibility. Panama has a rich cultural tapestry, including indigenous communities, Afro-Panamanian traditions, and influences from around the world.

1. Learn some basic Spanish phrases. Even simple greetings and "thank you" can go a long way in showing respect and building connections.

2. Ask permission before taking photos of people, especially in indigenous communities. Some believe that photographs capture a part of their soul.

3. Dress modestly when visiting religious sites or rural communities. This shows respect for local customs.

4. Support local artisans by buying authentic crafts. Look for items like molas (traditional textiles), tagua nut carvings, or Panama hats (which, interestingly, originated in Ecuador!).

5. Try local foods and drinks. It's a delicious way to support local producers and experience Panamanian culture.

6. Be mindful of cultural norms. For example, Panamanians often greet with a kiss on the cheek, but it's best to follow the local person's lead.

Economic responsibility is another crucial aspect of ethical tourism. By making thoughtful choices about where we spend our money, we can ensure that local communities benefit from tourism:

1. Stay in locally-owned accommodations when possible. This helps keep tourism dollars in the community.

2. Eat at local restaurants and food stands. Not only is the food often more authentic and delicious, but it directly supports local families.

3. Use local guides for tours and activities. They offer invaluable insights and ensure that tourism benefits local experts.

4. Be fair when bargaining. While negotiating is common in markets, remember that small discounts for you can make a big difference for vendors.

5. Tip appropriately for good service. While not always expected, tips are appreciated and can significantly impact local workers' livelihoods.

6. Be wary of voluntourism opportunities. While well-intentioned, short-term volunteer projects can sometimes do more harm than good. If you want to volunteer, research organizations thoroughly to ensure they have a positive, sustainable impact.

Let's talk about respecting local resources:

1. Be mindful of water usage, especially in rural areas where water can be scarce.

2. Use air conditioning sparingly. Open windows and use fans when possible to reduce energy consumption.

3. Properly dispose of waste. If there are no visible trash cans, carry your waste with you until you find an appropriate disposal site.

4. Respect local fishing regulations if you're engaging in sport fishing. This helps maintain healthy fish populations.

When visiting Panama's indigenous communities, additional considerations come into play:

1. Always visit with a reputable guide or through an organized tour. Many communities have specific protocols for visitors.

2. Respect privacy. Don't enter homes or take photos without explicit permission.

3. Be open to learning. These visits are opportunities for cultural exchange, not performances.

4. Respect traditional dress. It's not appropriate for visitors to wear traditional indigenous clothing as a costume.

Responsible travel also means being an informed traveler:

1. Learn about Panama's history and current issues. Understanding the context of the places you visit enhances your experience and helps you engage more meaningfully with locals.

2. Be aware of the environmental challenges facing Panama, such as deforestation and coastal development. Your choices as a traveler can impact these issues.

3. Stay informed about any social or political sensitivities. Avoid engaging in or supporting activities that might exploit vulnerable populations.

Consider giving back:

1. Look for opportunities to support local conservation efforts. Many national parks and protected areas accept donations.

2. Consider carbon offsetting your flights. While not a perfect solution, it can help mitigate the environmental impact of air travel.

3. Share your responsible travel experiences with others. Inspire fellow travelers to make ethical choices.

Responsible travel is not about perfection. It's about being mindful, making conscious choices, and always striving to leave a positive impact. Every small action counts.

By traveling responsibly in Panama, you're not just having a vacation – you're participating in the preservation of this beautiful country's natural and cultural heritage. You're creating connections that go beyond surface-level tourism, diving deep into the heart of what makes Panama special.

So, as you embark on your Panamanian adventure, carry these responsible travel tips with you. Let them guide your choices, enrich your experiences, and help you become not just a tourist, but a responsible global citizen. Your journey through Panama will be all the more rewarding for it, filled with authentic experiences, meaningful connections, and the satisfaction of knowing you've contributed positively to the places you've visited.

Chapter 8: Off the Beaten Path

Hidden Gems

While the Panama Canal and pristine beaches often steal the spotlight, this incredible country has so much more to offer. Let's embark on a journey to discover the lesser-known attractions and experiences that will make your Panamanian adventure truly unforgettable.

First, let's venture to the Azuero Peninsula, often called the "heartland of Panama." Here, you'll find the charming town of Pedasí, a hidden paradise for surfers and beach lovers. But the real gem is the nearby Isla Iguana Wildlife Refuge. This small island boasts powdery white sand beaches and crystal-clear waters teeming with marine life. Snorkel alongside colorful fish and sea turtles, or if you're lucky, spot humpback whales during their migration season. The island's limited daily visitors ensure a serene experience away from the crowds.

Heading inland, the mountain town of El Valle de Antón offers a cool respite from Panama's tropical heat. Nestled in the crater of an extinct volcano, this picturesque town is home to the rare golden frog, now only found in captivity. Visit the El Nispero Zoo and Botanical Garden to see these endangered amphibians. For a truly magical experience, take an early morning hike to the Sleeping

Indian Girl mountain. The view of the mist-covered valley as the sun rises is simply breathtaking.

Nature lovers shouldn't miss the opportunity to visit the Isla Bastimentos National Marine Park in Bocas del Toro. While Bocas is a popular destination, few travelers make it to Isla Zapatilla, two small uninhabited islands within the park. Here, you can enjoy pristine beaches all to yourself, spot nesting sea turtles, and snorkel in untouched coral reefs. It's like stepping into a Robinson Crusoe novel!

For a cultural hidden gem, head to the Emberá village of Parara Puru. Unlike some of the more touristy indigenous villages, Parara Puru offers an authentic glimpse into the Emberá way of life. You'll arrive by dugout canoe, learn about traditional medicines, watch artisans at work, and maybe even get a temporary jagua tattoo. The warmth and hospitality of the Emberá people will leave a lasting impression.

History buffs will be thrilled to discover the ruins of Panama Viejo. While not exactly hidden, these ruins are often overshadowed by the more famous Casco Viejo. Panama Viejo was the first European settlement on the Pacific coast of the Americas, and its ruins tell a fascinating story of conquest, piracy, and resilience. Climb the cathedral tower for a panoramic view of modern Panama City juxtaposed against these ancient stones.

For a truly off-the-grid experience, make your way to the Pearl Islands. Most visitors head to the popular Contadora Island, but the real magic lies in the smaller, less developed islands like Isla San José or Isla del Rey. Here, you can stay in eco-lodges, kayak through mangrove forests, and enjoy deserted beaches. The night sky, unpolluted by city lights, puts on a dazzling show of stars.

Coffee enthusiasts should plan a trip to Boquete, known for its coffee plantations. But instead of just taking a regular tour, why not participate in the coffee harvest? Some small, family-run fincas allow visitors to join in the picking process during harvest season (typically December to March). There's nothing quite like sipping a cup of coffee made from beans you've picked yourself!

Now, let's talk about food. While in Panama City, skip the touristy restaurants and head to the Mercado de Mariscos. This fish market transforms into a lively dining scene in the evenings. Head upstairs to the small restaurants and order a tower of fresh ceviche and a cold beer. It's where the locals go for the freshest seafood in town.

For a quirky experience, visit the Novia del Baru in Chiriquí. This "lover of the Baru" is a rock formation on the Caldera River that uncannily resembles a woman's face in profile, seemingly gazing at the Baru Volcano. Local legend says she's waiting for her lover to return. It's a great spot for a picnic and a swim in the refreshing river.

Adventure seekers should make their way to the San Blas Islands, but instead of staying on the more popular islands, arrange a camping trip to a remote island. Spend the night under the stars, surrounded by nothing but the sound of gentle waves. Wake up to a sunrise that will make you feel like the only person in the world.

In the Chiriquí highlands, the little-known Cerro Punta is a dream for hikers and nature lovers. This agricultural region is known as "the breadbasket of Panama" due to its fertile volcanic soil. Hike through cloud forests, visit strawberry farms, and enjoy the cool climate. Don't miss the Finca Dracula, an orchid farm named after the exotic Dracula orchid species it cultivates.

Finally, for a truly unique experience, time your visit with the Festival of the Diablos y Congos in Portobelo. This Afro-Panamanian celebration features dancers dressed as devils and African queens, telling the story of slave rebellion through vibrant costumes and rhythmic dances. It's a cultural spectacle that few tourists get to witness.

These hidden gems offer a chance to experience Panama beyond the guidebooks. They invite you to connect with nature, immerse yourself in local cultures, and create memories that go beyond typical tourist experiences. Each of these places holds its own magic, waiting to be discovered by the curious and adventurous traveler.

Remember, part of the allure of hidden gems is their unspoiled nature. Travel responsibly, respect local communities and environments, and help keep these special places pristine for future travelers to enjoy. Your journey through Panama's hidden gems will not only enrich your travel experience but also deepen your understanding of this diverse and beautiful country. Happy exploring!

Volunteer Opportunities

If you're looking to make a meaningful impact during your visit to Panama, you're in for an enriching experience. Volunteering not only allows you to give back to local communities but also provides a unique way to immerse yourself in Panamanian culture and connect with locals on a deeper level.

Panama, with its diverse ecosystems and vibrant communities, offers a wide range of volunteer opportunities. Whether you're passionate about environmental conservation, education, community development, or wildlife protection, you'll find a project that resonates with your interests and skills.

Let's start with environmental conservation, a critical area given Panama's incredible biodiversity. The Panama Amphibian Rescue and Conservation Project is doing vital work to protect Panama's unique frog species, many of which are endangered. Volunteers can assist in habitat maintenance, data collection, and even frog care. Imagine the thrill of helping to preserve species found nowhere else on Earth!

For those drawn to marine conservation, the Sea Turtle Conservancy in Bocas del Toro offers a chance to protect these magnificent creatures. Volunteers patrol beaches at night during nesting season, help with nest relocations, and assist in data collection. There's nothing quite like the emotion of watching tiny hatchlings make their way to the sea for the first time, knowing you've played a part in their survival.

If you're more inclined towards community development, consider volunteering with Fundación Calicanto in Panama City. This organization runs CAPTA, a program that empowers women from at-risk communities through vocational training and personal development. Volunteers can assist with English classes, computer skills workshops, or even share their professional expertise. The transformation you'll witness in these women's confidence and skills is truly inspiring.

Education is another area where volunteers can make a significant impact. Escuela Verde in the Chiriquí province combines environmental education with English language learning. Volunteers teach English to local children and adults while incorporating lessons about local ecology and conservation. It's a wonderful opportunity to shape young minds and foster environmental awareness.

For animal lovers, Fundación Yaguará Panama offers a chance to contribute to jaguar conservation. This organization works to mitigate human-wildlife conflict and protect jaguar habitats. Volunteers can assist with community education programs, help set up camera traps for monitoring, or contribute to habitat restoration projects. The thought of helping to protect these majestic big cats is thrilling!

If you're interested in sustainable agriculture, look into volunteering with Fundación Natura. They work on reforestation projects and promote sustainable farming practices. Volunteers can get their hands dirty planting trees, assisting local farmers, or helping with environmental education programs. There's a profound satisfaction in knowing the trees you plant will benefit the environment for generations to come.

For those with medical backgrounds, Health for Humanity runs mobile clinics in remote areas of Panama. Volunteers provide basic healthcare services to communities with limited access to medical care. The gratitude you'll receive from people who might otherwise go without medical attention is deeply moving.

Habitat for Humanity Panama offers opportunities for those interested in construction and community development. Volunteers work alongside local families to build safe, affordable housing. The joy of a family receiving keys to their new home is an unforgettable experience that will stay with you long after your trip.

If you're passionate about women's empowerment, consider volunteering with the Fundación Mujeres de

Éxito. This organization supports women entrepreneurs in rural areas of Panama. Volunteers can assist with business skills workshops, mentoring, or helping to market locally made products. Watching these women grow their businesses and support their families is incredibly rewarding.

For a unique cultural exchange, look into Sustainable Harvest International's volunteer program in the Darién region. This organization works with indigenous communities to promote sustainable farming practices. Volunteers live with local families, assist with agricultural projects, and gain deep insights into indigenous cultures. It's an immersive experience that will challenge your perspectives and broaden your worldview.

The Azuero Earth Project in the Azuero Peninsula focuses on reforestation and wildlife corridor creation. Volunteers can participate in tree planting, assist with environmental education in local schools, or help with wildlife monitoring. Being part of an effort to reconnect fragmented habitats and protect endangered species is incredibly fulfilling.

For those interested in urban development and social issues, Fundación Espacio Creativo in Panama City runs arts-based programs for at-risk youth. Volunteers can assist with workshops in music, dance, visual arts, or theater. The transformative power of art in these young people's lives is truly inspiring to witness.

When considering volunteer opportunities, it's crucial to choose reputable organizations that prioritize sustainable, community-led development. Look for projects that work closely with local communities, have clear goals and impact measures, and prioritize the transfer of skills and knowledge to local people.

Before committing to a volunteer project, ask questions about the organization's approach, the specific tasks you'll be doing, and how the project benefits the local community. Be honest about your skills and time commitment, and make sure the project aligns with your values and interests.

Remember, effective volunteering is about more than just good intentions. It requires cultural sensitivity, a willingness to learn, and a commitment to sustainable practices. Come with an open mind and heart, ready to learn as much as you teach.

Volunteering in Panama offers a unique opportunity to experience the country beyond the tourist trail. You'll forge deep connections with local people, gain insights into real-life challenges and solutions, and contribute to meaningful projects. Whether you're planting trees in the rainforest, teaching English in a rural school, or assisting with wildlife conservation, your efforts will have a lasting impact.

The memories you'll create, the friendships you'll form, and the personal growth you'll experience through volunteering will enrich your travel experience immeasurably. You'll return home with not just souvenirs, but with a deeper understanding of Panama, its people, and perhaps even yourself.

So, as you plan your Panamanian adventure, consider setting aside some time for volunteering. It's an investment that pays dividends in personal growth, cultural understanding, and the satisfaction of knowing you've made a positive difference. Your time in Panama will be all the more meaningful for it.

Unique Experiences

Welcome to the Unique Experiences section of our Panama Travel Guide 2024-2025! Get ready to discover some truly extraordinary activities that make Panama a one-of-a-kind destination. These experiences will not only create lasting memories but also give you a deeper appreciation for Panama's rich culture, stunning biodiversity, and incredible history.

Let's kick things off with an experience that's truly Panamanian - witnessing the Panama Canal in action from a perspective few get to see. While many visitors watch ships pass through the Miraflores Locks, you can take it a step further. Book a partial transit of the canal on a small boat. You'll feel the rush of adrenaline as your vessel rises and falls with the changing water levels, passing alongside massive cargo ships. The engineering marvel comes to life in a way that's impossible to appreciate from land. This thrilling journey through the world's most vital waterway gives you a front-row seat to global commerce in action.

For nature lovers, Panama offers a unique opportunity to witness the world's most awe-inspiring butterfly migrations. Between October and November, millions of butterflies cross the Isthmus of Panama. Head to the Metropolitan Natural Park in Panama City, where you can see swarms of yellow sulfur butterflies filling the sky.

It's a breathtaking sight that feels almost magical - like being inside a living, fluttering golden cloud. Timing your visit to coincide with this natural phenomenon offers a truly unforgettable experience.

Coffee enthusiasts, prepare for a sensory adventure like no other. In the highlands of Boquete, you can participate in a "seed to cup" coffee experience. This isn't your average coffee tour. You'll work alongside local farmers, picking ripe coffee cherries in the misty mountains. Then, you'll learn the art of processing, roasting, and brewing. The experience culminates in a cupping session where you'll taste the fruits of your labor. The depth of flavor in a cup of coffee you've helped create from scratch is unparalleled. It's a hands-on journey that will transform the way you think about your morning brew.

For a cultural experience that's both unique and deeply moving, visit the Emberá indigenous community in the Chagres National Park. Unlike more touristy indigenous experiences, this immersive visit allows you to spend a full day living like the Emberá. You'll arrive by dugout canoe, learn to fish with traditional methods, help prepare a meal over an open fire, and even get a temporary jagua tattoo. The Emberá's warm hospitality and willingness to share their culture create a profound connection that goes beyond typical tourist interactions.

Thrill-seekers, brace yourselves for the ultimate adrenaline rush - waterfall jumping in the lost waterfalls of Boquete. This isn't just about admiring waterfalls from afar. You'll hike through lush cloud forests, scramble over rocks, and then take the plunge from heights of up to 15 feet into crystal-clear pools below. The rush of flying through the air, followed by the refreshing plunge into cool water, is exhilarating. It's an adventure that combines natural beauty with heart-pounding excitement.

For a truly unique wildlife encounter, head to the Pearl Islands during whale watching season (July to October). But here's the twist - instead of just watching from a boat, you can actually swim with these gentle giants. Imagine being in the water as a massive humpback whale glides past you. The sound of their haunting songs reverberating through the water is something you'll never forget. It's a humbling experience that puts you face-to-face with some of the ocean's most majestic creatures.

History buffs and adventure seekers alike will be thrilled by the chance to hike the Camino Real. This ancient trail was used by Spanish conquistadors to transport gold across the isthmus. Today, you can retrace their steps on a multi-day trek through dense jungle, crossing rivers, and camping under the stars. As you walk, you'll feel a tangible connection to the past, imagining the challenges faced by those who traveled this route centuries ago. It's a physical challenge that rewards you with a deep sense of historical perspective.

For a taste of luxury with a uniquely Panamanian twist, indulge in a chocolate spa treatment using locally sourced cacao. At certain eco-lodges in Bocas del Toro, you can enjoy a massage using chocolate-infused oils, followed by a chocolate body wrap. The antioxidant properties of cacao are said to rejuvenate the skin, while the delicious aroma creates a multi-sensory experience. It's an indulgent way to connect with one of Panama's most famous exports.

Bird watching enthusiasts, prepare for an experience like no other - the Harpy Eagle encounter in Darién National Park. The Harpy Eagle, one of the world's largest and most powerful birds of prey, is notoriously difficult to spot in the wild. But in Darién, with the help of expert guides, you have a chance to see these magnificent creatures in their natural habitat. Watching a Harpy Eagle swoop through the forest canopy is a heart-stopping moment that will leave you in awe of nature's power and beauty.

Lastly, for a unique cultural immersion, time your visit to coincide with the Feria de las Flores y del Café in Boquete. This ten-day festival celebrates the region's flowers and coffee. But it's not just about admiring blooms and sipping brews. You can participate in traditional dances, join coffee tasting competitions, and even try your hand at flower arranging alongside local experts. The festival's vibrant energy and sense of community offer a joyous glimpse into Panamanian culture.

These unique experiences showcase the incredible diversity of adventures awaiting you in Panama. From heart-pounding thrills to profound cultural connections, from natural wonders to engineering marvels, Panama offers experiences that will challenge you, move you, and leave you with stories to tell for years to come. Each of these activities provides a window into what makes Panama special - its rich biodiversity, its fascinating history, its warm people, and its blend of tradition and modernity.

As you plan your Panamanian adventure, consider incorporating one or more of these unique experiences into your itinerary. They'll take you beyond the typical tourist path, offering deeper insights and unforgettable moments. Whether you're soaring through the air above a waterfall, locking eyes with a humpback whale, or sharing a meal with an indigenous family, these experiences will forge a personal connection with Panama that will stay with you long after you've returned home.

Conclusion: Embracing the Spirit of Panama

Panama beckons with its irresistible blend of natural wonders, rich culture, and modern marvels. This small but mighty Central American nation packs an incredible punch for travelers seeking diverse experiences in a compact package.

From the moment you set foot in Panama, you'll be captivated by its energy and charm. The gleaming skyscrapers of Panama City rise like a futuristic oasis, juxtaposed against the crumbling colonial architecture of Casco Viejo. This contrast perfectly encapsulates Panama's ability to honor its past while embracing the future.

But Panama's allure extends far beyond its capital. Venture into the lush rainforests, where howler monkeys serenade you from the treetops and colorful toucans flit through the canopy. Hike to hidden waterfalls, their crystalline waters cascading over moss-covered rocks. Keep your eyes peeled for the elusive quetzal, its iridescent plumage a prized sight for birdwatchers.

The archipelagos scattered along Panama's coastlines offer a slice of paradise for beach lovers and water enthusiasts. Imagine yourself lounging on powdery white sand, surrounded by turquoise waters so clear you can see straight to the coral reefs below. Snorkel alongside vibrant tropical fish, or catch a wave at one of the country's world-class surf spots.

For history buffs, Panama is a treasure trove of fascinating stories. Stand in awe before the engineering marvel of the Panama Canal, a testament to human ingenuity and perseverance. Explore the ruins of Panama Viejo, imagining the bustling colonial port town it once was. Uncover the legends of pirates and conquistadors that have shaped the nation's past.

Panama's indigenous communities offer a window into ancient traditions that have endured for centuries. Spend time with the Guna people of the San Blas Islands, learning about their intricate mola textiles and seafaring way of life. Visit a Emberá village deep in the Darién jungle, where traditional medicine and spiritual practices continue to thrive.

Food lovers will find themselves in culinary heaven. Savor the explosion of flavors in a bowl of sancocho, Panama's hearty national soup. Indulge in fresh ceviche at a bustling fish market, the citrusy tang perfectly complemented by an ice-cold local beer. Don't miss the chance to sample artisanal chocolate made from some of the world's finest cacao, grown right here in Panama.

Adventure seekers will find no shortage of thrills. Zip-line through the rainforest canopy, heart pounding as you soar above the treetops. White-water raft down rushing rivers, navigating rapids with expert guides. For a truly unique experience, embark on a multi-day trek through the Darién Gap, one of the most biodiverse and challenging environments on Earth.

Panama's commitment to conservation is evident in its vast network of national parks and protected areas. Coiba National Park, a UNESCO World Heritage site, protects pristine coral reefs and provides a safe haven for endangered species. The cloud forests of Volcán Barú National Park offer unparalleled hiking and the chance to glimpse rare wildlife.

While Panama's natural beauty is undeniable, it's the warmth and hospitality of its people that truly make the country shine. Panamanians take pride in sharing their culture with visitors, always ready with a smile and a helping hand. You'll find yourself drawn into lively conversations, invited to impromptu dance lessons, and treated like family in small towns and big cities alike.

When planning a Panamanian adventure, remember that responsible travel is key to preserving this incredible destination for future generations. Support local businesses, respect wildlife and natural habitats, and be mindful of your environmental impact. Seek out eco-friendly accommodations and tour operators committed to sustainable practices.

Learn a few basic Spanish phrases before you go – even a simple "gracias" goes a long way in showing respect for the local culture. Take the time to really connect with the places you visit and the people you meet. Ask questions, listen to stories, and immerse yourself in the rhythms of Panamanian life.

Panama's diversity means there's truly something for every type of traveler. Whether you're seeking relaxation on pristine beaches, heart-pumping adventures in the wilderness, or cultural experiences that will broaden your horizons, you'll find it here. The country's relatively small size makes it possible to pack a wide range of experiences into even a short trip.

As you leave Panama, you'll carry with you memories that will last a lifetime. The vivid colors of a Caribbean sunset, the thrill of spotting a resplendent quetzal, the satisfying exhaustion after a challenging hike, the laughter shared with new friends over a home-cooked meal – these moments will stay with you long after you've returned home.

You'll find yourself daydreaming about your next visit, eager to explore the corners of the country you didn't have time for on this trip. Panama has a way of getting under your skin, calling you back again and again.

Get your sense of adventure, open your heart to new experiences, and get ready for the journey of a lifetime. Panama awaits, ready to surprise, delight, and inspire you at every turn. Your Panamanian adventure starts now – what are you waiting for?

Made in the USA
Columbia, SC
30 December 2024